M000286380

RECRUIT MY KID!

A Parent's Guide Thru the Recruiting Process

Thank you…

Jacquie for your love, support and gene pool. Without those three things—I would not be me, could not have attempted this project (again), and would not have a 6' 7" son, a 6' 2" son and a 6' 4" daughter!

To my friends and family who suffered through reading the earlier drafts.

To UNC, OSU and PSU Compliance

Special Thanks to…

Noretta Roberts (Mom) – who refused to allow her one and only child to be "just" an athlete – your legacy continues in the lives of Brennan, Camren, and Jaylen. #STUDENT-athletes

Uncle Harvey for making me finish.

BMW, Cam, Jay and (Mani) – for allowing me to ride along with you all. I am proud of you – "you guys gettin' there!"

My friend, brother, pray partner and of course Editor (extraordinaire) Terry E. Carter for turning my MESS into a MESSAGE!

To the Next Generation of great athletes – through NextGen & The SHOW! we are changing the world "one athlete at a time"!

Apologies to…

Those who are mentioned in an unflattering light. In order to educate the readers, my (brutally) honest interpretation of our experiences were necessary.

THANK GOD!

In the Beginning...

Over the past several years I have had the great pleasure of speaking to student-athletes across the country, sharing how sports have impacted me and my family. I speak at football camps, basketball tournaments, high schools and even middle schools. I have been featured on national radio, TV, and in print. Much to my wife's chagrin, the title of my message to these impressionable young minds is "Athletes Rule the World!" That's right, I have the audacity to say that athletes *rule* the world. I am not saying that it's right or that it's fair – but if we are honest with ourselves, we have to admit that we are a society fixated on sports.

We pay more attention to our favorite teams than we pay to the economy or world affairs. Our families gather around major sporting events. We proudly wear the colors of our favorite teams. We argue, debate and (unfortunately) even fight over our alliances with our teams. The ratings for Lebron's "Decision" captured almost 10 million viewers. The Superbowl is practically a national holiday. In fact the ratings for the game once doubled the ratings for a US Presidential debate in a highly contested race. Sports can bridge racial gaps, socioeconomic differences, politics, and religious affiliations. It is that passion for sports that led me to coin this phrase and stand behind my message with such confidence.

As a former professional athlete, sports have had a tremendous impact on my life. But that's only part of the story. My business degree has provided the foundation for my life after football. While it was my ability to play football that paid for my education, it was my education that allowed me to become a Sr. Vice President and Managing Partner in a successful investment advisory firm. However, I'd have to admit that the door to the financial world was opened because I was a former pro football player. I often struggle with this dichotomy. I have come to the realization that it is not a "chicken or egg" situation, but rather a "hand in glove" situation, where sports helped me get an education and opened career doors for me. Then, my education allowed me to grow and flourish in the business world.

It's easy to see that being an athlete has benefited me, but a deeper look shows how it has impacted the lives of my children.

Those of us who love sports also love to live vicariously through others. So, while I played at the highest level of my sport – I still enjoy sharing the experiences of my kids' athletic endeavors.

I introduced my sons to the game that I love, football. However, I steered my daughter toward my favorite sport (unbeknown to most), basketball. Unfortunately, my basketball career was hindered by my growth. I stopped growing "upward", but I kept growing "outward." That development forced me to the gridiron.

My oldest son Brennan started playing football at the age of seven, in our town's Pop Warner football league. Having grown up in Flint, Michigan, I was a product of a school youth football program that produced three NFL players. Growing up in a tough city where sports were viewed as the vehicle to get to live the "good life", I wanted my son to love the game that had brought me so much joy. Little did I know that his introduction to the game on that hot summer night in August, in the small town of Easton, Massachusetts, would set him on the same road that I had traveled many years before him. Although it was the same road, with hopes of the same destination, the road had drastically changed. I wrote the first edition of this book to share my story through Brennan's experience, hoping to provide direction for other parents who feel as lost as I did. As I proudly completed *Recruit My Son – A Father's Guide Through the Process of College Football Recruiting,* I thought my work was done. I expected to go through the process with my second son Camren and my godson Armani – but I did not expect the landscape to have changed so quickly. Before the ink was dry in my first edition, it seemed almost obsolete. What's more, when I my daughter received her first recruiting letter from a

4

college basketball program in 7TH grade, I knew I was in trouble. I had absolutely no clue about the intricacies of (women's) college basketball recruiting. Beyond this, it was happening at the same time that the (younger) boys were being recruited. I knew how much time, energy and resources (translation: "money") I'd put into Brennan's recruitment. Now our family was being confronted with three college recruitments simultaneously.

I wish I could simplify the process and tell you that recruiting is the same for all sports. I wish I could say that there are the same number of scholarships for both male and female student-athletes (in every sport at every college). I wish there was a streamlined and consistent recruitment process that could easily be understood by the average parent. Unfortunately, a magical genie has not granted me these three wishes. So understanding the complex collegiate recruiting process remains challenging to say the least.

My ultimate goal as a young football player was (as with most young players) to make it to the NFL. However, playing in a city that has produced hundreds of professional athletes – my immediate goal was to make the youth football team a Dailey Elementary. If asked I'd bet that most NFL players were probably never overly concerned about making their youth football teams, but most NFL players didn't have to battle with the likes of Carl Banks (Giants), and Lonnie Young (Cardinals) to get noticed on the field. Furthermore, in a small city like Flint that produced the likes of Pro Bowlers Andre "Bad Moon" Rison, Superbowl hero Mark Ingram, and "Big" John Runyan (Eagles) – you really had to compete for honors and accolades that most NFL'ers never have to consider. Although the three of us (Carl, Lonnie and I) made it to the highest level of football, we often joke that were weren't even the best players on our school team. Guys like Darryl Washington, Dorman Freeman and Jon Frye were the stars on the Dailey Elementary roster. Unlike my battle for playing time and attention – when my son Brennan walked on the field for the first time at age 7, he was noticeably bigger than his 8, 9 and 10 year old teammates. When he got

5

into his three point stance for the first time, he looked as if he had been playing football for 10 years. Although he had been around football all of his life, he had absolutely no clue about how to play the game. But he was a sponge and just about everything he was taught he mastered quickly. When I taught him to drive block, he would push players all over the field. When I explained how to tackle, pull and trap, or cut block, he would naturally execute the techniques like a wily old veteran. From the first time he walked onto the field I knew he was a special talent, and that it would be my job as his father-coach to help develop this gifted child into a college football player.

Whether you are Earl Woods, Jack Elway, Joe Bryant, Kellen Winslow, or Richard Williams, developing a young athlete is very challenging. I use those examples as *extremes*, but gifted young athletes are rare; and if you are reading this book, you (at least) suspect that your son or daughter is a gifted athlete with the possibility of a future in college sports.

Unlike Brennan's first days in Pop Warner, Camren walked on the field with a different "swagger". Camren had been the team's ball boy for 2 years while anxiously waiting to play. Since there's not a lot for a ball boy to do on a Pop Warner team, he participated in drills with the older boys. He knew all of the plays and was literally another (albeit little) coach on the field. When Cam was finally allowed to play – it was almost unfair. Here was a kid who was playing with other youngsters who had never played before. His football "IQ" was at least 2 or 3 years ahead of most of the team. He was extremely well-coordinated and very fast. It was a lethal combination for that level of play. He played running back on offense and his first 3 carries in the team's initial scrimmage were 60, 60, and 45 yard touchdowns. He also played defensive back and was a ferocious hitter. Because Pop Warner rules require 7 year olds to play at the instructional level, Cam was forced to play with kids who weren't at his level. I compare it to putting an advanced third grader back into kindergarten.

Regarding this recruitment process, I've jokingly refer to my kids as "projects." My eldest, Brennan was project #1. Younger brother Camren and godson Armani are project #2 and #2.5, respectively. And my youngest, daughter Jaylen, is lovingly referred to as project #3.

To this day, I struggle with project #3. My daughter Jaylen is arguably the most physically gifted athlete in our family. Just under 6' 4" in height, she has a wingspan of 6' 10". She can run and she can jump. I mention these particular attributes because girls are different. Quite often girls have the physical attributes to play, but don't have the athleticism to excel. Jaylen truly looks the part. So much so, that her first *unofficial* offer came from Providence College after seeing her in the pre-game warm-up line prior to an actual game. Even more surprising. she played all of 6 minutes, scoring 2 points, grabbing 2 rebounds, and blocking 1 shot. These are hardly impressive statistics, nor would one think they are

worthy of a Division 1 scholarship offer. So how do you motivate, inspire, or challenge an athlete who can just "show-up" and be coveted.

This book will address the recruiting process from several perspectives. We will provide directions that will apply whether your athlete is a Division 1 prospect, or simply a great student who loves the game and is playing for an opportunity to attend a desired college.

Whether you knew it when your kid was 7, or if you just figured it out as they turned 17, *Recruit My Kid* can help you. If your athlete is a physical specimen, an athletic "freak", or just a hard-working kid that's passionate about playing at the next level. read on.

Be mindful and remember this book is not a road map. Instead it's a GPS to help you navigate you through the "PROCESS" of planning and preparing for a college student-athlete. I use the term GPS rather than road map because proper use of a road map requires knowing where you are as you begin a trip. Conversely, technologically-advanced global positioning systems (GPS) – don't require that you know where you are. They only need for you to know your destination. So set your mental GPS to your child's COLLEGE SPORT, and then follow the twist and turns, ups and downs. I am confident that you will get there safely. One warning, **don't blink**! It goes by so quickly. Remember, enjoy every sight and scene along the journey.

The format of this book is set up like a game. We'll start with game planning through each quarter (or phase) and into overtime, and believe me there will be overtime. The Game Plan section is where you will have to do some research – as you will need to understand the strengths and weaknesses of your kid's individual skills, their high school program, AAU, club teams, and the recruiting landscape in your region of the country.

Upon completion of your "recruiting game plan", you will move from quarter to quarter, learning from both my successes and failures. Recognize that some lessons apply to all sports, while other are only applicable to your sport. Each quarter focuses on a specific segment of the process that I feel is required to navigate from *"where you are" to "where you want to be"*. Lastly, the overtime section addresses special situations and circumstances that may apply to your unique recruiting situation.

As you read this book please remember that I am a "coach". I have the heart of a coach, I view life from a coaching standpoint. Whether you are overseeing your family, a congregation, a youth sports team, a professional football team or managing a Fortune 500 company you are a Coach! The best definition of the word Coach that I have ever heard was Joe Ehrman a former professional football player and current high school coach. He goes back to the origin of the word "coach" – (picture a stage coach) where a coach is a vehicle designed to carry and protectively cover someone of importance from point A to point B. More specifically take someone from where they "are" to *their* destination. As a parent of a gifted student-athlete you have been entrusted to "coach" through the ups and downs of their experience to reach their goal and destination.

So get your note pad and let's get ready to embark on this incredible journey.

Game Plan

Before the first quarter begins, which is when you introduce your child to the game or sport, you need to have a game plan. Biblical wisdom, says that a wise man considers the cost before he starts to build. In order to consider the cost, you must have a plan in place. Coaches meet for hours and hours to decide the plans for each week's upcoming game. They look at their team and their opponent to devise a strategy that will effectively accomplish their goal – to win the game. Obviously, these plans don't always work, because both teams in the game have prepared a game plan, and one team still loses. However, one adage is correct when it comes to game planning. "If you fail to plan, you are planning to fail."

The story is told about Jack Elway, John Elway's father – who recognized his son's athleticism while he was in first grade. Earl Woods knew that Tiger was destined for greatness, and began to map out his future at the age of two. My biggest concern in referencing stories like these is the unbelievable pressure some parent is going to put on their five year old son the first time he drops a ball while playing catch. It is important for parents to be supportive, but realistic.

Like every father's dreams, when I pictured my first son following my football footsteps, I envisioned him being a running back like Emmitt Smith, the name on his first football jersey; or a quarterback like Kordell Stewart, his second jersey; or maybe a defensive back like Ronnie Lott. As amazed as I was with Brennan's potential as a lineman, I was equally shocked by his inability to run fast like Emmitt, or throw like Kordell, and he couldn't catch or cover like Ronnie. As a runner he was slow.

He was big for his age and was as clumsy as a newborn giraffe. I often joked that he couldn't "run out of sight" in three days, or I'd kid with him and say that he couldn't "catch a cold, sitting on a block of ice in an igloo". Humor is a big part of our family, and we love to "crack-jokes" on each other. These jokes or wise cracks were not to demean or hurt him, it's just how our family communicates. Thin-skinned (or sensitive) people don't hang around our house too long.

As a defensive lineman, I was always frustrated with not getting the opportunity to play a "skill" position – like quarterback, running back, defensive back or wide receiver – which in football are the "glory" jobs. As a football player I was considered exceptional. My "measurable" statistics were 6' 4 ½", with a playing weight was of around 280; and I ran the 40 yard dash in 4.79 seconds. My wife was also an athlete. She was a high school high jumper and played volleyball. She was also a professional runway model standing a little over 5' 10". So it was natural for me to assume that my son would be tall. Furthermore, because of the combined athletic gene pool, I didn't think it was too much of a stretch for him to be extremely coordinated. I always wanted a son who would run for the touchdowns that I didn't in my career. But this kid (Brennan) didn't have any of the skills to play any of those "skill" positions. In fact, if you saw him play at one of those positions you would think that this kid had absolutely no future in this sport. Still, if you put him on the offensive line and told him to block someone, or put him on the defensive line and had a player try to block him – you would quickly see the same thing I saw. You would see a dominating blocker who could block anyone, and a defensive lineman who couldn't be blocked. The complexity of football allows many types of athletes to have success.

Much to my dismay, over the years I have noticed more and more young athletes foregoing football for what I refer to as the "S" word, SOCCER. Because of soccer's increased popularity, football has lost a lot of potential players. As a youth football coach competing for kids in our small town, I tried to instill pride in those young men who chose to play football. I'd would tell them how tough they were, and how "soft" soccer players were. I would refer to football players as "steel" and soccer players as "cotton". *I have great respect for the athleticism of soccer players, but I was desperately trying to keep my potential running back and receivers from defecting to the youth soccer program.* To further complicate things, Easton is not what anyone would call a "football" town. The high school football program has struggled, while our soccer program is pretty highly regarded.

I wanted our football players to view themselves as the cream of the "athletic" crop – making them think that the best athletes played football, and if you weren't good enough, or tough enough, *then* you played soccer. I know these comments and antics sound extreme, but I was trying to change a paradigm.

Although Brennan didn't have the skills to be a receiver, or run fast enough to be a running back – he could BLOCK! Our (town's) youth football practice field was adjacent to the more popular youth soccer field, and I developed a phrase – "make'm play soccer" – after he literally drove a kid off the football field, down a hill, and slammed him onto the soccer field. His opponent quit football that night, and joined the town's soccer program the next week. The mindset of the football program was changing!

As with any football game, preparation for the game planning process is where you identify your strengths. As a parent of a potential college athlete, your first job is to recognize what position he is best suited to play. This is important because if he is going to play the game, he has to learn to love the game. If he loves the game he will be willing to put in the work to improve and develop his skills. The best way to get your son to love the game is to put him in position (literally and figuratively) to succeed. Too many dads ("daddy-ball) want their sons to play a position that they are not built to play, which leads to frustration when "little Johnny" can't catch, or run. But they (will still) put "little Johnny" at running back or wide receiver. Then after a year or two watching their son endure failure after failure, and deal with the teasing and ridicule of his peers – the child quits and chooses another sport, or even worse he quits all sports, and loses his desire to compete. Nothing upsets me more than "so-called" knowledgeable football parents who fail to put value on linemen. I've had fathers who I've coached with, pull their sons off the team, or refuse to allow me to coach their son, because I felt their son was a "lineman". Recognize your son's gifts, and find a position that allows him to use those talents. You should also realize that kids grow at different rates. I have coached players who were linemen when they were eight or nine years old, who evolved into running backs or defensive backs in their high school years. One of my close friends (former Patriot teammate), Wide Receiver and World Class Hurdler Michael Timpson, credits his toughness as a receiver to playing guard during his Pop Warner days. Minnesota Vikings Hall of Fame Guard Randall McDaniel, was a high school All-American Fullback. Jevon "The Freak" Kearse, an All-Pro Defensive End, was a high school Safety. If you support your son's great blocks and recognize his contribution, he will learn to appreciate whatever role the coach gives him.

Game planning for basketball is much different. A basketball team may have more than one game per week. In planning, just as in the actual sport, things happen faster and they happen sooner. I shared earlier that my daughter received her first letter from a college in the 7th grade. Crazy as it sounds, there are *actually* national recruitment ratings services that list and rank kids as early as 4th grade. In this regard, basketball players have several venues to showcase their skills – from Amateur Athletic Union (AAU) programs and club teams, to scholastic competition and showcase camps. Since elite basketball players are easier to identify, the recruiting process starts much earlier. When you see a kid in 6th grade that stands 6' 3" – like one of my former AAU players, Nerlens Noel (2013

NBA Lottery Draft Pick) – you get the notion that this is going to be a college basketball player.

Further complicating matters, across the spectrum of team sports, individual player roles also make for very different recruitment scenarios. Even as an experienced pro athlete, I learned (the hard way) that Brennan's recruitment as an offensive lineman was different than Camren's recruitment as a defensive back/ linebacker and Armani's recruitment as a wide receiver/ defensive back.

Recognizing these differences in recruiting by sport, and even by position within a given sport, is mission-critical. You really need to have an understanding of the distinctions.

Over the past few years I have been invited to speak, share and educate student-athletes in a lot of different sports. I love spending time researching and diving into the recruiting intricacies of different sports as I prepare for a specific sports speaking engagement. I have spoken to baseball, softball, volleyball, track and field, soccer athletes, as well as football and basketball groups. While it was clearly my job to educate my audiences, I actually learned a great deal while preparing.

Don't take the preparation stage for granted! You're reading this book, so maybe you've got that piece down already.

The reason I love the game of football so much is that it takes players of different sizes, different speeds, and different skill proficiencies and brings them together to play the ULTIMATE team sport.

There are a ton of variables that will come into play as you continue through the Game Planning process. As I reached the point where the recruiting process had become a second "full-time" job, I came to realize that there are parents all over the country who don't understand this process. Moreover, if I, someone who had been through the recruiting process, felt lost – parents who've had no exposure to this experience must feel really lost. Furthermore, living in a state where the overall experiences with high level college football recruiting are limited, caused me additional anxiety.

My anxiety grew when I was confronted with basketball recruiting and even moreso when I realize that recruiting for top-flight *girls* college basketball was even more challenging.

My job has now evolved from "Parent-coach" to "Parent-Coach-Manager" (PCM). As a PCM, I realize that I have put countless hours into getting my kids exposed to college programs, managing the information we receive from these programs, and fostering and developing relationships with schools who share our (my wife and my) vision for the type of programs that we want to consider.

So let's take a step back for a moment…On average there are about 10 players each year from the state of Massachusetts who receive scholarships to NCAA Division 1 football programs. Compare this to "mega football" states like Florida, Texas, California or Ohio – where literally hundreds of players each year are offered and accept Division 1 scholarships. On the other hand, basketball recruiting in our region tends to produce college players fairly consistently. Still, there are not a lot of Bay State players who attend elite Division 1 programs. Part of understanding your teen's recruitment strengths and weaknesses is identifying whether or not your state, city and child's school has experience with the scholarship athlete process. **This is critical!**

It is clearly important for you to know how your state (and region) is viewed as a breeding ground for talent in your child's sport. If you live in a state that frequently produces college athletes in **their sport**, it is very likely that your child's *school* has had exposure to the process and can help you navigate your way through the maze you're entering. I highlight the words **their sport** because some areas may be known for producing high quality athletes in (let's say) football, but they don't have a lot of experience with baseball or track prospects. Due to the unique issues within the recruiting process of each sport, it's important to know your school's experience. Beyond this, you have to look at the process from the college's prospective. I was talking to a Bill Kenney, a former offensive line coach and area recruiter from Penn State, during Brennan's Junior season. He explained that colleges recruit with a budget – and not just a financial budget, but a time and resource budget. By NCAA rule, football coaches are only allowed 2 visits to your son's school from April 15th to May 31st. So if you don't live in an area that has a lot of highly touted prospects – coaches may not have the time or resources to visit your son's school. "Why would I go to Massachusetts to see two or three players, when I can go to Florida and see 50," Bill explained.

Take football for example. Realizing that the limited number of players being recruited from our state was an additional "barrier to entry," I began early on to map out how to get my son Brennan some exposure. When Brennan was in elementary school and playing in the Pop Warner program, we began looking for private schools in the area that played Division 1 high school football (the state's highest level). The high school in our town of Easton, MA had a smaller Division 3 football program. This football program was also going through a transition and there was a lot of turmoil. Understanding the landscape of your son's school's football program is very important. The last thing you want is to put your son in a program that is unstable, and not prepared to coach/develop your son's skills. This may not be an issue in your state, but in Massachusetts it presents a challenge because of the limited number of players who are recruited to play at top colleges.

Quick Story: "Same Kid, Different Zip Code

A good friend Steve Burton, a local Sportscaster reached out to me for advice regarding his son Austin's recruitment. Steve (a former college football player) and his wife Ginni have four athletically gifted children and all four have received Division 1 scholarship offers, three in women's basketball and Austin as a Quarterback in football.

Steve had grown (very) frustrated with the recruiting process because he felt Austin was being penalized because he was playing high school football in Massachusetts. I explained to Steve that Quarterback was (and is) the toughest to get a scholarship offer. And that he had to get him outside of Massachusetts – to show that Austin's skills measured well against kids from the elite recruiting States. After putting up huge numbers as a Sophomore – Steve took my advice.

Austin did visits and went to camps at Boston College, Duke, North Carolina, Michigan, Colorado, Steve's alma mater Northwestern, competed at the Nike Elite 11 regional competition, and countless other showcase events. After a great Junior season, where Austin received All-Conference, All-State awards – Steve and Ginni continued to expose Austin to the top QB camps, school visits and events.

Still frustrated with the lack of offers, Steve and Ginni took my "get him "outside of the State" advice to another level. Midway through Austin's Junior year the family made the tough decision to allow him to transfer to a high school in Orlando, Florida and live with relatives. My recommendation was just for camps and competitions – (laughing) I didn't mean "move the boy".

Austin was immediately immersed in to Spring football and won the starting QB job after throwing for nearly 400 yards and five touchdowns in the school's Spring game. Numbers that were very similar to the numbers he consistently put up back in Massachusetts. News began to spread (back) to the schools that had so far shunned the gifted QB.

Following the successful Spring, Steve began to take (*the same*) Austin to many of the same camps, colleges and events – and received shockingly different responses. Austin received his first Power Five Conference offer from Boston College.

BOSTON COLLEGE, SERIOUSLY! The campus of Boston College (BC) is less than 10 minutes from the Burton family home in Massachusetts. Austin had visited the school and met with the staff countless times. Moreover, he had attended their elite camp each year. **And now they offer!** What was different? **NOTHING!** Did he have a huge growth spurt? **NO!** Were his numbers markedly better in Florida? **NO!** Within days of the BC offer he received offers from UCLA, Tennessee and Colorado. The same kid that "couldn't get a sniff" now had four Division 1 offers.

Austin recently committed to UCLA. Same kid, different zip code!

(Back to Brennan)

After my wife and I decided on a school with good academics that played Division 1 football, I began to "choreograph" his football camp schedule. Brennan attended several football camps throughout his elementary days (See Camp Section), but in the 8th grade I began to focus on skills related, non-contact camps. He was allowed to attend the Boston College (BC) Football Camp as an 8th grader, because he was going to play Freshman football. Ordinarily the BC camp is limited to high school players, so I viewed it as an opportunity for him to play with bigger and older kids, in a controlled environment.

My plan was to put him into one camp as an 8th grader, and for him to do two camps as a 9th grader. Because BC was the closest "D-1" school, I planned to have him attend their camp every year. BC has a great reputation for developing good offensive linemen, and I wanted him to become very comfortable with the school and the staff. I felt this was important. After all, if BC (the local school) didn't show interest, how could I ever expect Penn State or Michigan to recruit him. In the 9th grade he attended two camps, the BC camp and Penn State. The summer before his Sophomore year, he attended BC and Syracuse. I would love to say that they fell in love with him and offered him a scholarship immediately, but they didn't. But remember, at this point that was not the goal. My goal was to get him familiar with camps and give him the opportunity to compete with kids from different states. I never allowed him to buy into the idea that players from Massachusetts were inferior to kids from other states. And, because he had confidence in his abilities, he felt comfortable displaying them wherever he went.

As he continued to develop, we had to take our exposure schedule to the next level -- destination NIKE CAMP! Brennan completed his Sophomore year as the only player to start on both offense and defense. He started at Right Tackle (offense) and Left Defensive Tackle. The season came to a challenging close, with the team record of 1 – 9. But we put together a highlight reel, and obtained a recommendation letter from his head coach and athletic director. We sent the tape to NIKE and requested early admittance to the Nike Football Training Camp.

The Nike Camp is held in the Spring and is traditionally for Juniors. I felt if we could get him into the camp a year early *I felt* he'd be on his way!

After several anxious weeks we received the news. He was accepted and received a formal invitation to attend. He attended the camp and did a great job. More importantly, he did a great job in front of 50 or 60 Division 1 football programs. The camp was held at Penn State, and attended by coaches from schools like Notre Dame, Michigan, Maryland, and Syracuse. Currently NCAA rule prohibit coaches from attending these types of events, however they are heavily covered by scouting services and media who disseminate the results to college coaches and recruiting staffs.

The camp consists of two parts; beginning with basic agility drills that focus on the movements and skills related to each player's position. The second part and highlight of the camp are the one-on-one drills. These are the drills that separate the *mere* attendees from the "playa's". I refer to really gifted kids as "playa's". Having lived in the Boston area for over 20 years – its quite common for native Bostonians to yell out, "wow that kid's a playa". I guess it sounds better when you drop the "r". But *you'll know* if your son is a "playa"!

I have always been amazed that at every level there are players who shy away from competition – players who have worked in the weight room, conditioned their bodies, are invited to camps, given a scholarship, or even drafted – who choose to hide in the back of the line rather than compete. I have always shared these thoughts with Brennan, telling him to watch for these players when he goes to camps, or plays on teams. They are everywhere! Well, lo and behold, they were at the Nike camp hiding among the mere 300 invitees.

As the coaches set up the for the one-on-one pass rush drill, I noticed several players in Brennan's offensive line group, (players) who looked phenomenal during the **non-contact** skills and agility drills, but who literally hid in the back of the lines to avoid the competition against the invited defensive linemen. Each offensive lineman is expected to get two or three chances against the defensive linemen. Brennan had seven attempts, meaning that others didn't get any. It wasn't that he was being greedy, just that he was willing to try. One of the first books I gave Brennan was by the great Michael Jordan, entitled "I Can't Accept Not Trying". I don't know if it was the book or if it was innate, but he has never backed away from trying. Actually he was probably too naïve to be afraid to compete.

The defensive linemen have a tremendous advantage in the one-on-one pass rush drill, mainly because they know it's going to be a pass. Besides this, the drill is challenging without pads (full equipment), because it eliminates some of the techniques offensive lineman can use. In a setting like the Nike Camp, against some of the best defensive linemen in the country, winning one out of three would be good. Two out of three would be great. Brennan won six out of his seven attempts.

As we walked off of the field feeling great about his accomplishments – a coach approached and introduced himself. His name was Chris White, a coach/ recruiter from Syracuse. He shook my hand and told me that he thought Brennan was a scholarship athlete, and to get ready to hear from Syracuse.

The week after returning from the Nike Camp, Brennan's high school coach received calls from 10 or 15 schools, who were surprised to hear that he was just a Sophomore. The game plan was working great!

Unlike my high school to college football recruiting experience, *my son* had to rely heavily on exposure events like the Nike Camp. One key reason was the lack of players who were being recruited from Brennan's school, conference, and Massachusetts all together.

When I was a Junior at Flint Northern High School in Michigan, there were seven Seniors from my high school that received D1 scholarships. In addition there were probably 10 to 15 other prospects from our conference. This provided me with a tremendous platform for exposure. As coaches would scout my teammates or conference opponents they would also see me play. Four players from my Senior year team moved on to play D1 football; and it was considered an off year. By comparison, a good year in Massachusetts means that 10 to 12 players (from the entire state) receive D1 scholarships.

These numbers are very important for you to know. Using the prospect search engine on sites like Rivals.com, Scout.com, 247 Sports, or ESPN Recruiting, you can find out the number of players who have moved on to play college football at the Division 1 level.

After a week or so **away** from training and football (altogether), Brennan resumed his dual training regimen. Brennan trains with his high school teammates three days a week, and with EPS Training in (nearby) Foxboro, MA, three days a week. I feel it is important for him to train with his high school teammates, because he is one of them. As a leader, his work ethic will hopefully inspire others to work hard. Furthermore, he needs to let his teammates know that they are important to him. He trains with the director of EPS, Brian McDonough – who trains several professional athletes. Current and former New England Patriots' players like Adam Vinateri, Jarvis Green, Troy Brown, Wes Welker, Randy Moss, and Rob

Gronkowski rave at the results that they have obtained through Brian's unique training program. Through Brian, Brennan has had the opportunity to work out with some of the current Patriots, and it has helped him recognize how much work goes into playing the game.

I decided to write the first edition of this book after being approached by several of my son's high school teammates (and their parents) who wanted to know more about the recruiting process. They also wanted to know how Brennan went from being a little known prospect from the smallest Division 1 high school in the minimally recruited state of Massachusetts, to one of 90 players selected to participate in the most prestigious High School All-American game in the country, the US Army All-America Game. How did Brennan become the first offensive lineman in the history of the state and third player from Massachusetts to receive this honor? Many would say it's his name (having a father who played in the NFL); some would say it's his measurable (at the time) – standing 6' 6 and weighing 275 pounds; others would say that he's a heck of a football player. I would love to believe it is solely the latter, but honestly there are a lot of worthy players who were not selected. Although he **is** a heck of a football player, Brennan has been exposed nationally, which has allowed him to be seen by the" who's who" of high school football talent evaluators – Mike Farrell and Jeremy Crabtree from Rivals.com, ESPN's Tom Luginbill, JC Shurburtt from 247Sports.com, and Brandon Huffman, Jamie Newberg, and Chad Simmons from Scout.com. Furthermore, athletes looking for early attention, need to know Al Popadines of Youth1.com. No one is more knowledgeable on the top middle school (yes I said middle school) prospects in the country. Lastly, and certainly not least, the *great* Tom Lemming – recognized as THE AUTHORITY on high school football players. You may not know these names now, but if you are serious about getting your son to the next level in football – YOU BETTER!

Furthermore, be mindful that you won't have the luxury of waiting until your athlete's Sophomore or Junior year to get started – college coaches are identifying athletes earlier and earlier. In fact, my NextGen Camp Series has produced more than 300 division 1 offers to MIDDLE SCHOOL athletes.

For girls basketball I had to learn about influential analysts and reporters like Bret McCormick from the All-Star Girls Report, Keil Moore of Prospect Nation, Joe Fenelon of NYG Hoops Report, the "Godmother" – Lisa Bodine of Blue Star Media and ESPN's Glenn Nelson. ESPNW covers women's basketball extensively. There are also countless individuals who cover and report on boys basketball prospects and recruiting. If your son is looking at division 1 basketball, I recommend you follow Eric Bossi – Rivals.com, Evan Daniels and Brian Simon – Scout.com, and Dave Telep – ESPN. Whatever your kid's sport, there are key people that you should know and follow. And in the age of social media – you can literally follow them minute by minute. Assertively following the "who's who" of scouting in your son or daughter's chosen sport is not as "creepy" as it may sound. Rather it offers you key insight into what events they cover and their coverage schedules. In addition, most seasoned observers regularly give recruiting updates, with information like which coaches are attending which events. Another valuable service they provide is individual player ratings and rankings. I will discuss the importance of this last service in greater detail later in the book.

I have heard the "gripes" from people in Massachusetts about my kids and their recruiting successes. Many suggest that because I played for the Patriots – doors were opened for my boys. They also say that my knowing people in recruiting circles has given my kids an advantage. Could my kids have benefited from my name or access? Absolutely! Nevertheless, I am confident of this simple fact – if they weren't talented, they would not have been offered scholarships.

Let's do a small math exercise to prove my point. One of the schools that offered athletic scholarships to all of my kids is Boston College (BC). BC is one of the top academic institutions in the country. The cost to attend BC is about

$50,000 per year. Over a 4 or 5 year college career that's the can amount to $250,000. Schools don't **give** $250K to a kid whose dad is a former pro player, unless that kid can help their program. Beyond this, let's consider the case of Hall of Famer Jerry Rice, one of the greatest football player in NFL history. His son Jerry Rice Jr. was a (non-scholarship) walk-on at UCLA. At the end of the day, the scholarships go to the best and most well-suited athletes to the recruiting school's program needs.

Let's take another look at Brennan's recruitment. Most football fans, even many in New England, don't know who Brent Williams is, or that he (I) once played for the Patriots. So I really don't think that was the reason for Brennan's notoriety. That being said, though I'm proud of my Marketing Degree from the University of Toledo, I recognize that it "ain't" from Harvard! There definitely is something to a name, but's it's not everything. I have told many folks in a variety of different situations that the product being marketed has to work. Stated another way, Ivory spends a ton of money marketing its soap; but if your hands aren't clean after you use it, people won't buy it. It's the same with Brennan. I took him to a bunch of college camps, sent him to the Nike Camp, and the All-America Combine. I put together highlight films for schools, and created a bio/resume and sent it to coaches. But at the end of the day, "the soap worked." Each time he walked off of the field, he had made an impact and left an impression on those who saw him. *I say all of that to say this*, be careful of marketing a product that doesn't work. Too many fathers hear how Tom Brady's dad sent film to Michigan, and think that, "if I could

just send my son's film to Michigan they will love him and he'll become the Super Bowl MVP."

I would love to say that every school I sent film to offered Brennan a scholarship. Actually we chose to send his Sophomore highlight film to 20 schools, and we heard back from 16 of them. The strategy for film will be outlined in detail later in the book. But there were several schools that we sent film to, that we didn't really care about. We simply recognized the value of any exposure their interest might offer.

Admittedly the focus of this book is on Division 1 recruiting. However as you read though this material, my hope is that it is NOT only viewed as a guide to getting your son or daughter into a Division 1 program, but also as a guide for those interested in getting their child to the next *appropriate* level of their chosen sport. There are 120 Division 1 programs that have 85 football scholarships each to offer to student-athletes. They usually have about 20 – 25 new scholarships per year. Considering that there are more than a million high school football players in the United States, it's fairly clear that not everyone is a "D1" player. Therefore it's also important to understand that there are about 200 Division 1-AA who offer 63 equivalents (like scholarships) each, as well as roughly 170 D2 schools that offer 36 equivalents, as well as the opportunity to play in Division 3 or NAIA for those athletes who want to play after high school.

To take it a step further, there are more than 300 Division 1 basketball programs, that usually offer between 1 and 5 new scholarships per year. In addition to "D1" opportunities, there are more than 200 Division 2 and Division 3 schools. Remember the goal is to get funding for your son or daughter's education using their athletic gifts as the vehicle. A listing (by sport) of the number of key athletic programs at every competitive level is provided in the back of this book.

A good friend, Ric Anderson, who I coached with, taught me the "line of the century" when it comes to scholarships. Ric and his son Julian were weighing options during his football recruitment. Julian chose to attend the University of North Alabama. UNA is a Division 2 school with a rich football tradition. They offered Julian a partial football scholarship (50%), along with an academic scholarship that covered another 30% of his tuition. Lastly, Ric, as a retired firefighter, qualified for financial aid that covered the last 20% of Julian's educational expenses. When the recruiting coordinator presented the package to the Anderson family – he began to apologize for not being in a position to offer Julian a "full athletic

24

scholarship". Ric cut him off with what has become my all- time clinching statement in my speaking engagements. He told the coach, "Listen there is NO need to apologize – I understand business! You can call it an athletic scholarship, an academic scholarship, (hell) you can even call it a grant, AS LONG AS YOU DON'T CALL IT A BILL, **I'LL TAKE IT!**" Now that was spoken like the parent of three boys who were all in college at the same time.

Another of my favorite recruitment experiences revolves around a player named Nick Cataldo. Nick was a player I coached in 2007 and a very good football player. More importantly, Nick was a great student. He had a 3.85 GPA in all Honors and Advanced Placement courses. He also scored 1890 on his SAT. Nick applied to one of the top academic schools in the country, Bowdoin College in Maine, which *US News and World Report* and *Newsweek* both refer to as one of the "New Ivies". During the interview process, Nick was advised NOT to include his impressive SAT score, but rather to get a letter from his football coach stating his willingness to play football for the school. Nick was accepted and a received a great education while continuing to play the game he has loved since childhood.

As the NCAA commercial states, "most college athletes turn pro in something other than their sport." Nick has now *turned pro* and is working for one of the nation's largest sports marketing firms. Although the majority of my focus is on D1 recruiting, the *real* intent of this book is to help guide your quest to get your son or daughter the opportunity for a quality education. More importantly, I want to see you get funding for the ever increasing costs for that education. NCSA Recruiting Network advances research showing that more than 90% of college scholarship opportunities fall outside of Division 1. If pro sports is in your kid's future, that's great. But let's be clear, he or she will still need an education. That should be the *specific* destination for which you set your GPS.

Remember, good grades and great SAT (or ACT) scores are not enough anymore. Colleges are looking for more.

They want well rounded, diversely talented individuals that can contribute significantly to their campus community. Although it does not currently apply to most athletes – many schools are in fact moving away from including standardized tests like the SAT and ACT as a part of the admissions process. As with Nick, it was his abilities as an All-Conference Lineman that "supported" his great academic record. If sport becomes the tool that supports your child's college application, they (still) have to be a good player at the competitive level of their chosen institution – even if that choice can't realistically include top-tier, D-1 programs.

I wish I could tell you that the recruitment road travelled for Brennan was the same one I used for Camren and Armani – but I can't, because it wasn't. There were a lot of similarities, but because of their differing positions on the football field, we had to get each athlete exposure in other ways. Because Cam and Armani both play at the skill positions, high school games and camps weren't enough. Another key strategy was to attend a number of 7 on 7 skills competitions to showcase their abilities.

7 on 7 tournaments are an increasingly popular way for skill players to demonstrate that they have the abilities to play at the next level. 7 on 7's are football games played without linemen. They include quarterbacks, running backs and receivers competing against linebackers and defensive backs in a two-hand touch football competition. These events are aggressively covered by the major scouting services and offer an indirect path to scholarship opportunities. 7 on 7's are quickly becoming the football version of basketball's AAU or soccer's club teams. There is a great deal of concern about these games, as the NCAA resists any unsanctioned activities where prospective athletes can be exploited. To say they are concerned is actually an understatement. As my granddad would say – "they are as nervous as a long-tailed cat in a room full of rocking chairs". In this instance, I believe that the NCAA's fears are legitimate. I've seen for myself that, just as in the AAU,

some of the individuals attached to these events are in it for personal gain.

In this regard, basketball is literally another world. AAU Teams are often funded by major sneaker companies like Nike, Reebok, Fila and Adidas. When you mix multimillion dollar companies with youth sports, the results can be less than desirable. I'm not going to this book there, as we might lose sight of our destination. I simply ask that you understand the landscape of your child's sport – know all of the platforms where your sport can be seen and impacted. Please closely review the "Places to Be List" in the back of the book to find out where your student-athlete needs to go to be *seen*.

High School basketball is great! The school spirit, passionate rivalries, and the feeling that you are playing for something bigger than yourself are just a few things that I love. The AAU, however, is a completely different animal – it has become THE biggest platform for high school basketball players to display their skills. As the largest individual showcase for colleges to find talent, AAU has literally and figuratively changed the game of basketball. Instead of referring to the AAU by it's real name, Amateur Athletic Union – I call it what is really is… **ALL ABOUT U!** It has become one of the most sinister and treacherous sports platforms in youth sports. That being said, AAU participation has in many ways become a necessary evil for parents that want their kids to play college basketball.

The critical part of the AAU season begins at the end of the normal high school basketball season. Starting in March, the AAU season extends through the Fall (pre-HS basketball) season. One key reason that AAU competition is so important is that it coincides with both the NCAA's official April and July "Live" College Viewing periods.

During your son or daughter's high school basketball season, colleges are also competing. As such, collegiate programs are focused on winning their own games at this time. They are practicing, meeting, scouting, preparing and travelling for games. Consequently, they may not have the time and resources to simultaneously scout prospective talent. Trust me, college coaches do their best to manage all facets of their jobs – but it's really challenging. With that understanding, the AAU season allows coaches to see a lot of talent in a short period of time.

Whether it's schoolboy/girl sports, club competition, AAU, or travel team play, understanding the entire landscape of your child's athletics will significantly impact the outcome of your success in this journey.

So now that we've gone over all of the pre-game material, it's "game time!" Once last reminder before we move on--please remember. As you embark upon this journey, "don't blink". While our family and friends joined together to watch the 2013 NFL Draft, waiting anxiously for Brennan's name to be called, I began to reflect. My reflection was not on his college years at North Carolina, nor his high school years. So as the phone rang and the Houston Texans informed Brennan that he was going to be their next draft pick and as cheers exploded in the room, the tears streaming down my face were not from elation on the next phase of his football experience, but rather from remembering the first time he ever put on a football uniform.

As you read through this book take some time to remember and reflect on the beginning.

1ST Quarter: The Love of the Game

As previously stated, I have two sons, Brennan and Camren. I also have one daughter, Jaylen. One of the things I had to learn about my boys is that although they both love the game of football, they love the game differently. When Michael Jordan was asked to identify the most important trait in developing young basketball players, he quickly said, "teaching them to love the game." He explained that if they love the game they will be willing to put in the work to improve their skills.

At an earlier age, my younger son Camren studied the game every Saturday and Sunday. He watched the game looking for ways to improve his play. He was always asking questions like, "do you run a post pattern differently against cover two than against cover three." Things like, "dad that guy should have sat down on that route, because the defense was in a zone," were common comments from Camren. As a high school player he would talk with his coach about plays that the team should run, and his opponent's strengths and weaknesses. After his games, he would come home and play catch, or work on a pass that he dropped during his game. He ate, drank, and slept football. His love for the game continues to pay dividends – as he became the first Scout to be hired directly from college by the New England Patriots. A job that requires him to (literally) eat, drink and sleep football six to seven days a week – and up to 16 hours a day. I was always told that if you love your job, you will never work a day in your life.

One Christmas, Camren asked for a Jugs Football Passing machine to work on catching in the off-season. I explained that he could just work with the two candidates for quarterback. He rebutted "they play baseball in the Spring." He also explained that if he could catch fast balls from a machine that shoots balls 100 yards, he could catch anything from any quarterback.

On the other hand my son Brennan (the big time All-American) watched about two football games a year, mainly the

Michigan-Ohio State game, and the Superbowl. It's a family tradition to watch Michigan play Ohio State and EVERYONE watches the Superbowl. To be honest, I think he watched the Superbowl for the commercials. As he the college recruiting process began he was forced to watch more games, or at least know the scores of the schools that were recruiting him. Coaches would

call each week and would ask if he had seen their game, and what he thought about their play. I often found myself acting like the President's Chief of Staff, providing him with weekly "briefings" on the various school's game results so that he could sound informed and interested.

The reality is Brennan's love of the game differs from Camren's. Brennan loves to compete. He loves playing in games. He loved being recognized as one of the top players in the country. He loved the camaraderie he shares with his teammates. That love drove him to work out. That love drove him to eat right. That love drove him to go to bed early, when everyone else is "hangin' out". And that love made him study film, instead of playing with his Playstation.

Then there's Jaylen! I'll just start by saying girls are different than boys. I firmly believe that what drives and motivates them is a lot different from what drives and motivates most boys. Jaylen absolutely loves basketball! However, what she loves about basketball is the attention she receives from being one of the top players in the country. She is very competitive, but not necessarily with her peers. She competes with her brothers. She is proud that she received her first letter from a college recruiter in the seventh grade, a full three years before her brothers got similar notice. She wanted to win a High School State Championship mostly because her brother's never did. I think she also loves the sport of basketball because it's her dad's favorite sport and it's different from what the boys are known for. She is motivated because she loves her team, her teammates and coaches. She is driven because she doesn't want to disappoint her team. She recently shared that she is also fueled by the fear of making Penn State look bad for recruiting her. Those are the things that push her to practice really hard, and to do extra work with a personal skills coach Claude Pritchard.

The point is, not everyone loves the game the same way. Your son may or may not like watching football at every waking moment. He might love other aspects of the game. Your daughter may not like basketball the way you want. Find out what motivates them and appreciate their differences. Allow them to grow as individuals in the game and their love for the game will also grow.

I watched Brennan go from a kid who barely watched film or studied the game into a young man who is truly professional and genuinely appreciates his craft. He learned that he had to become a student of the game to play at the highest level. He recently stated in an interview that he "had an awakening after his sophomore year of college." He came to the realization that he would not enjoy the level of success he had become accustomed to if he didn't change his approach. He said "I realized that I couldn't (just) rely on my intelligence (classroom) and natural talent (football field) to carry me any longer. I learned to study harder in both school and football. And my performance improved tremendously."

The wake-up call for Jaylen also came during her Sophomore year. For most athletes natural talent and God-given ability will only carry so far. Great players become great, because the WORK!

Recognizing Talent

In my 40 plus years of football, as a player, a coach, and as a father, one of the biggest issues I have struggled with is the failure to recognize whether a player has the talent to play the game. I have always used the word talent because I believe it encompasses everything it takes to play the game. Skills + Toughness + Desire = Talent. This equation looks and works much better than the (potential) acronym.

31

In every sport there are a set of skills that must be evident in order to effectively compete at the collegiate level. Moreover, no matter what sport your son or daughter plays – they must have a level of toughness and desire if they are going to become a successful collegiate student-athlete.

As a coach I have been approached by a number of parents who believed their child was a talented athlete. There are a lot of players who have one or two of the big three attributes, but they're not the total package. I am sure you've seen players that have skills, but lack toughness, or desire. More common are players who have toughness or desire, but don't have the skills.

It is possible to get to the next level without all three, but those guys who stick out as the "greats" in our memories had all three. In my years in the NFL, I came across countless players who lacked in one of these critical areas. Rarely (if ever) was the missing ingredient skill. Don't get me wrong, I've had quite a few teammates that did not have the talent to compete in the NFL, but usually players lacked in the other two areas. Players who lack in the skills area are usually "weeded out" before reaching the ultimate level. However, some players have SO MUCH skill that they are able to advance without having toughness and/or desire.

In today's 24 hour news cycle, you would have to live under a rock not to see the lack of character (let's call it the big "C") in professional, collegiate and even youth sports. In the first edition of this book, I named specific examples of individuals who had made mistakes that caused their character to be questioned. There are countless athletes who have demonstrated that they lack character – and it's not just the "run of the mill" player, but many at the top of their profession. Take a moment and google "athletes who have had _____"…You can fill in the blank with legal issues, steroid problems, domestic abuse, drunk driving, and a host of other challenges. Although athletes are celebrated as if they are super human, they are NOT. They make the same mistakes in the same areas that non-athletes do…the same mistakes that plague our society as a whole. The difference is, to quote the first Spiderman movie – "with great power, comes great responsibility". The power of an athlete's platform for the positive is magnified exponentially when it comes to the negative.

Just as it is in other areas of life, it remains true that the biggest names in sports, despite character issues, still manage to make it. The fact that such folks are household names is evidence that you can make it to the next (if not the ultimate) level without the big "C". Still, I believe that there will come a day when character will play a larger role in determining whether a player makes it to the next level. For now, there will be numerous athletic programs that will accept student-athletes with questionable character. However, elite collegiate programs that offer high quality educations – steer clear of "bad" kids. Furthermore, everyday we are seeing more athletes dismissed from sports programs when they fail to comply to with rules once they arrive on campus.

While we are on the subject of character, I have always believed that poorly behaving players didn't become jerks when they made it to the pros. I'd contend that the guys responsible for the negative headlines were "turds" when they were kids! But because they were so talented, no one ever corrected their bad behavior – so now millions of professional sports fans are punished, because some parents and (youth) coaches failed to put him or her in their place.

My experience suggests that the character issue in basketball is a huge challenge. I think this is due to the fact that basketball players are recognized as "special" at an earlier age – an age where they may not be mature enough to handle special treatment or attention. Most observers knew Lebron James was going to be great when he was in 7th grade. A kid who is 6' 5" in junior high will be treated differently than a kid who is 5' 6". I am not saying that it "right" or "fair". The facts are the facts. Due to her physical attributes, my daughter received attention from colleges long before her basketball skills warranted their letters and scholarship offers.

You can improve skills with practice. You can encourage toughness, and desire can be enhanced by developing the aforementioned love for the game. You can even correct poor behavior – and develop character. But the fact remains (as my high school coach used to say), you can't make "chicken salad" out of "chicken sh*t". In other words, you can't make a kid who runs a 6.4 forty-yard dash run a 4.6. Basketball coaches always say "you can't teach height". I am always careful to say "improve" skills, not make something out of nothing (or very little).

My two favorite (current) NBA players are Lebron James and Steph Curry. Obviously Lebron is a physical freak, but he continues to develop his game year after year by working at his craft. While Steph is built like a regular guy. I believe his popularity is enhanced because people see him as a guy who works incredibly hard. Both are amazing talents but Steph is more relatable.

Although basketball is my favorite sport, the differing physical attributes which can lead to success in football is why I love that game so much! The skills required to play the game are so diverse that a wide range of athletes can play. In football, players with different heights, different weights, fast guys, and/or strong guys can all be successful. I wouldn't describe Tom Brady or Peyton Manning as fast, but they are great players. In this new era of more athletic quarterbacks, guys like Cam Newton and Russell Wilson are able to play the same position differently, but very successfully. All the coaching and skills camps in the world would NOT have made Brennan a running back or quarterback. He can't run like a running back, or throw like a quarterback. And the sad thing is that I see so many fathers try to make their kid a quarterback, when the youngster is clearly not skilled in this area.

I guess this is as good a place as any to address one of my biggest pet peeves – coaches who put their son in at quarterback. Over the years I have noticed a trend in youth football, where the son of one of the coaches is chosen to be the team's quarterback. I this current "Daddy-Ball" era of youth sports, too often, the kid's only qualification is that he is the son of the decision maker. Obviously there are exceptions to *"my rule"* – we *do* hear of NFL quarterbacks who are "coach's kids", but I believe these occurrences should be very *rare*.

Several years ago I went to a coaching clinic and learned how to choose a quarterback for a youth football team. The first question the presenter asked was how many fathers in the room had a son who played quarterback for their youth team. More than half of the dads in the room raised their hands. Do you honestly believe that almost 70% of those kids had the wherewithal to play QB? I don't! The speaker said it's a huge mistake to make your son the QB unless he fits the following criteria.

1. One of the smartest kids in his class (hopefully the smartest)

2. One of the toughest kids in his class

3. Someone who excels in other sports

I found it interesting that he never mentioned a great arm, or great speed, and he never mentioned a high football IQ – things that I would have thought important for making the selection. But, after thinking about the most successful QB's that I had coached they all fit the bill. They were smart, tough, and good in other sports.

Their intelligence was important because that's how kids identify leaders. They gravitate towards kids who are smart in school and although they may not like or hang out with the "smart" kid, they *will* have respect for his academic success. Toughness in a QB is also very important because (even in youth football) the QB is the face of the team. If he is easily rattled, the whole team is affected. I use to joke with my coaching staff that "if your quarterback cries, the team will die." Lastly, the only thing that kids respect more than a smart kid is someone who is GREAT in other sports – not good, GREAT! If your son excels in other sports he will gain the admiration of his peers. If he is a great baseball player or extraordinary basketball player he has a chance to become a quarterback.

My experience with female athletes has shown other significant differences. Their positive off field/court attributes are magnified. I am sure you have seen the commercial suggesting that girls who participate in sports are more likely to be successful academically, socially, and professionally.

Beyond this, female athletes tend to be gifted in multiple sports, like basketball players that also excel at volleyball, or field hockey players that can also do it on the ice. One of the challenges that will be addressed in this book is the pressure to specialize or play only one sport early in their athletic careers. Exceptional female athletes tend to stick out like a sore thumb. I suspect that if you are reading this book with your daughter in mind, you already know that she's a gifted athlete. It's just a matter of what sport she'll play and what level.

I have counseled several female athletes entering their high school years that excel in two or even three sports. When I say excel, I mean EXCEL! They are legitimate scholarship candidates in more than one sport. I think it's great that these girls have choices – as with many facets of life, the more options one has, the more leverage they possess.

Fundamentals

Whenever you hear about a team struggling to perform well, you may hear the coach suggest that the solution to their problems is to "get back to the basics." This phrase is uttered at every level of football from Pop Warner to the NFL. From the town recreation league to the NBA and from the high school track to the Olympic stadium—getting back to the basics simply means focusing on fundamentals – the fundamentals of any competitive game or athletic pursuit.

As you work with, or look for someone to develop your child's skills, make sure that the focus is on developing strong fundamentals. Fundamentals are the proper execution of the techniques for the position within the sport that he or she plays. Sometimes when a quarterback throws an interception, it is because he misread the defense, but most often it is because he didn't use the proper technique. The reality is that football is a pretty simple game. It is based on running, blocking, tackling, throwing, and catching in a coordinated, cohesive manner. These basic activities are performed best when the proper techniques are used. As amazed as we are by the incredible physical feats we see in college and professional basketball, the best players all have strong fundamentals. Great runners – run more efficiently than average runners. Every sport has a set of actions that are "fundamental" to successful participation. The better your son or daughter becomes at the fundamentals of their sport – the more likely they are to excel.

As a member of the NE Patriots Alumni Club, I am permitted to attend practices. I am amazed at the amount of time that coach (Bill) Belichick spends on fundamentals. Basic tackling drills, footwork for the quarterbacks, and simple catching drills by the receivers are repeated over and over. The reason that great teams stay great is because they stress the basics.

When we were searching for an AAU program for my daughter – we chose a program that focused on fundamentals. During our search, we met with several coaches and we *entrusted* her to the Rivals Basketball Club, coached by Scott Hazelton, largely because of his focus on fundamentals and developing offensive skills. This will be discussed in more detail later in the book.

The reason why I put this section in the book is that so many parents and coaches are looking to see their young prodigies execute the spectacular, that they omit developing basic skills. It's the reason I tell the *(boys)* youth basketball team that I coached to watch women's college basketball instead of men's basketball – because the women's game is not focused on superhuman dunks, circus-worthy shots, and one-man gangs, it's based on sound fundamentals and team principles. Too often we see young players catch the ball with one hand, and we never refocus them on the importance of getting their bodies into the proper position to catch the ball with both hands. Young basketball players watch ESPN highlights, and the marvel at dunks and three-point shots. Too often, more basic basketball skills, like the art of mid-range shooting, go unnoticed.

During a practice in my rookie year with the Patriots – I witnessed one of the most amazing acrobatic catches by an incredible athlete. Former number one draft pick (wide receiver) Irving Fryar made a one handed catch that required him to out-jump a defender and literally change directions while in mid-air. Everyone watched the play with sheer amazement, but among the *oohs, and ahs* there was one unimpressed voice, Hall of Fame Wide Receiver Raymond Berry our Head Coach, who yelled "two hands while learning." Coach Berry meant that in his professional opinion the one-hand catch was unnecessary and the catch should have been made with two hands. Early in his career, the thing that made Irving special was his ability to make the spectacular grab, but what made him a concern was how he performed the routine catches. And his career sputtered until he mastered the routine.

The Hall of Fame Wide Receiver Cris Carter had a saying during his career. He said, "a great receiver catches everything that he's supposed to, and some of the balls he's not supposed to." The focus is on the basic or the routine, not the extraordinary.

Make sure your kid can execute the basic tasks of their position or sport using good technique. Almost every sport requires the ability to *run*. When running, make sure he or she runs properly, using both arms and legs in balance. Make sure they change directions the right way by planting on their outside foot, so that they change directions efficiently. Most importantly, make sure that the person coaching them understands the fundamentals and is adept at teaching them. At the end of day, it will be their fundamentals that get your athlete to the next level.

Respect the Game

Although it doesn't *always* seem like it, the professional sports leagues spend millions of dollars on researching their players' backgrounds. My former teammate Marvin Allen, who worked 12 and 5 years respectively in the New England Patriots and Atlanta Falcons college scouting department, and is now the newly appointed Director of College Scouting for the Kansas City Chiefs, tells me that they interview high school coaches, youth coaches, teachers, and everyone they can to learn about a player's character. The extra due diligence has paid off, the Patriots (until recently) and the Falcons rarely have off the field issues with their players. As the amount of money invested in players goes up, I believe more time will be spent assessing character. One way I measure character is by how much a player respects the game.

In this "selfie" age of (often shameless) self-promotion, big ME – little team, I often feel embarrassed by some of the antics of players in the pros. While I'm not naïve and recognize that the media plays up negative behavior for some and downplays it for others, bad actors are out there. Nor is selfishness, spoiled, and self-centered behavior limited to wide receivers and defensive backs. There are quarterbacks who display a lot of these undesirable traits. Generally the quarterbacks are not viewed as divisive, like the Chad Johnson's and Terrell Owens' of the game. What worries me about the trends I see in the games I love is not *just* the antics of the players of today, but their failure to respect the game.

Early in my NFL career I was humbled by a conversation I had with Raymond Berry where he explained that the things I was allowed to do on and off the field were provided by my football-forefathers – those who played without helmets, without big contracts, and without the benefits of the modern day luxuries. He wanted me to understand that it was their literal blood, sweat and tears that I was standing on. Moreover, I would have to someday give an account for the gift and abilities that I had been blessed with, more importantly with how I used those gifts.

We try to link the next generation of great football players to the history of the game by inviting the top 100 performers in grades six through nine to the Pro Football Hall of Fame for the largest youth football showcase in the country – The SHOW. The SHOW allows the top players in the country to compete against each other – with the Hall of Fame as the backdrop. We tour the Hall and have Hall of Famer's speak to the kids (hoping) to connect them to the history of the game.

I believe that if the players of today, who seem to think the game is "all about themselves," could grasp the fact that are merely baton holders who will pass the game onto the next generation, their respect for the game would deepen. No matter how big the player, how great their personality, how dominant the abilities, the game goes on long after they are gone.

Teach your son or daughter to respect their game or sport! If the player respects the game they will respect their coaches, the officials, and their opponents. This important concept has to be introduced to your athlete at an early age. If it isn't engrained in their competitive persona, it will become a (bigger) issue as their talents become more in demand.

Will schools recruit "_ _ _ holes?" Absolutely! It's unfortunate, but it's true. So the only deterrent is **you,** correcting the behavior before it becomes an issue at the next level.

Academic Base

Because of my experience as a former professional football player who has witnessed the college recruiting process first hand, many have asked my advice on how to help themselves, a child, or a talented prospect they know. In the beginning, I would dive head first into evaluating their film, and putting together a plan to market the player's abilities. Researching (by sport) which exposure events they should attend. Furthermore, I would spend hours on the phone attempting to link them with colleges I thought would be a good fit. One of the biggest mistakes I made was the failure to analyze the prospect's academic performance. After being burned (countless times), the first thing I now ask for is a copy of the kid's transcript. You see, it is very easy to get caught up in the excitement of a talented young athlete, but we have to remember that they are STUDENT-ATHLETES! And, in order to get into a college they must pass the NCAA Eligibility Center guidelines. Meaning they have to have decent grades or their athleticism is "all for naught."

A little later on, I will go into the details on the process of registering for the NCAA Eligibility Center and the steps required to become a viable scholarship athlete candidate.

It is critical for you to recognize academic strengths and weaknesses as well as athletic strengths and weaknesses. Too many coaches, parents, and administrators gloss over academic weaknesses and fail to properly prepare young men and women (especially young men) for the challenges they will face in the class and examination rooms.

As your child grows to love their sport, make sure you establish consequences and punishments for poor academic performance Beyond this, always look for ways to support those areas where they struggle. Like Mr. Goodwrench (in the old General Motors commercials) would say, "you can pay me now, or you can (really) pay me later." If you don't provide guidance in the discipline area it could cost you a scholarship.

As Brennan grew to love playing football more and more, he knew that he had to maintain at least a "B" average to continue playing. More importantly, he knew that my wife and I weren't bluffing. We were serious about his academic performance. This focus on academics was instilled in me by my mother, who *despised* the "dumb jock" moniker many athletes wore. At a very early age, she would point out poorly done interviews and the "duh, duh, duh" responses from what she viewed as unintelligent athletes.

Education always came easy to Brennan. On the other hand, Camren struggled in his early elementary years. He required additional academic support in order to keep up with his classmates. In addition to the added "in-school" help,

Camren attended the local Sylvan Learning Center to address areas missed by me, my wife and his teachers.

Through these extra efforts, he developed study skills, self-discipline, and turned into a phenomenal student. He was a Distinguished Graduate and a three year member of the National Honor Society. He finished his first year at Ohio State on the Dean's List and was named to the Academic All Big 10 Team each of his four years of college — a long way from the kid who struggled through second and third grades. Camren graduated from Ohio State in three and a half years with a 3.5 gpa.

While your kid doesn't have to be a straight "A" scholar to get into a D1 school, he or she does have to be a decent student. To be candid, the academic requirements for qualifying for most D1 athletic scholarships are pretty pedestrian, which makes the fact that so many players fail to qualify, even more tragic.

2ⁿᵈ Quarter: Skill Development

Skill development is one of the (if not **the**) most critical areas of this process. I have always been a huge fan of fundamentals, and I recognize the importance of developing skills that allow you to perform at *your* highest level. The emphasis is on "your", because "your" child's highest level may not match another kid's highest level. I love the old Ladainian Tomlinson commercial for Nike products – saying "My better is better than your better!" As a parent you must realize that your son's fastest 40 time may not be as fast as his buddy's best. Your daughter's top vertical jump may not match another girl's best. Your son or daughter may not be as strong as another player, or as physically gifted. That's where skill development comes into play!

Name the greatest receiver to ever play football… That's right, it's Jerry Rice! Jerry was NOT the fastest receiver to ever play, nor was he the tallest, or strongest, or greatest in any other physical attribute. But he was the best! Why? Because he was the most skilled. He ran great routes, he understood coverages, and knew how to get open. He outworked everyone! Jerry ran the 40 yard dash in (a very average) 4.65 seconds, but he was more skilled than faster wide-outs. Because he realized that he couldn't outrun everyone, he decided that he would train his body to run his fastest 40 yard dash time (4.65) – 40 times in a row. He noticed that the guys who ran the super fast 4.2's and 4.3's didn't have a lot of endurance – and although they could run a 4.3, 40 they could only do that one or two times. By having a high level of endurance, Jerry looked a lot faster than guys who were actually faster than he was.

In 1993 we were preparing to play the 49ers and Hall of Fame Coach (Bill) Parcells explained to our defensive backs (who would have to cover Jerry) that they were not allowed to show fatigue. If they even looked tired – Rice would give the QB (Steve Young) a signal to throw a deep pass for a touchdown. Our cornerbacks practiced "controlling their breathing" the entire week, never leaning on their knees or showing weakness. We lost the game that day, but our defensive backs did a pretty good job containing the greatest receiver ever.

Part of skill development is learning how to camouflage your weaknesses. Jerry Rice had great hands, ran great routes, and was a tremendous competitor – but he had to learn how to hide the fact that he wasn't the fastest guy on the field.

As I watch my kids play sports, I look for things they don't do well. I love finding weaknesses in their games. When we find a weak spot in their abilities or skills we are one step closer to "greatness".

As I mentioned before, I grew up in the state of Michigan – and I was a HUGE Magic Johnson fan. So at a very early age I learned to love "Magic". Of course, if you love Magic, you hate (Larry) Bird. Still, as much as I disliked Bird (growing up), I recognized that he was incredibly skilled. He wasn't fast and couldn't jump (high), nor was he the strongest guy on the floor. But he was an incredibly talented basketball player. Rarely did you notice how "slow" he was because he knew how to hide his deficiencies.

Your kid should aspire to be the best that they can be. If that "best" is good enough for him or her to become a D1 student-athlete, that's GREAT! If their best opens the door for them to get a solid education at a top D3 school, then that's GREAT too!

Two of the toughest decisions I've had to make were in this area of skill development, more specifically in the building of fundamentals. Years ago I started my own AAU program. The boys I started with were 4TH graders and coached them through the 8TH grade. As they approached the 8TH grade, I began to realize that the serious basketball players needed more than I was able to offer. It was really hard for me to face that my time had run its course with these young men. I knew that a kid like Nerlens Noel (now an NBA pro) needed more than I could give him. Not just from a coaching standpoint, but also from an exposure standpoint. He needed to be in a high profile club setting that would offer him access to an elite AAU schedule that my small program couldn't provide. I sent Nerlens to the Boston Amateur Basketball Club (BABC). BABC is a Nike-sponsored club that boasts a list of prestigious alumni, like Basketball Hall of Famer Patrick Ewing. Nearly every great player over the past 30 years has been a part of similar top-level club organizations.

The second tough decision hit a little closer to home, it was with my daughter Jaylen. Just as with my boys group, I had started a very successful girl's team when she was in 5TH grade. Having gone through Nerlen's development – I knew that there would reach a point where I would have to pass her on to a more experienced coach and program. But it was my daughter for goodness sake, my "favorite athlete", "daddy's little girl" – and was I really going to entrust her to someone else? This is a common mistake that I see parents make. Oftentimes you've been your son or daughter's first coach and there will come a time when your son or daughter may outgrow your coaching acumen. As hard as it may be to admit, your kid may need to another coach or program to take them to the next level. Sometimes it happens sooner than we'd like; nonetheless it remains one of the biggest failings I see in youth sports. Understand that it's not always your lack of knowledge either. Quite frankly, sometimes your kid just needs a break from you. Your voice gets old. They get tired of hearing you say the same things over and over. This is where it became a challenge for my ego. I had to be willing to let another coach take Jaylen to the next level. In doing so, I found that our relationship improved both on and off of the court. As the head of my own program, I was responsible for the entire team. When Jaylen left to join the Rivals Basketball Club with her new coach, it was a huge relief. For the first time I was (just) a parent watching her. Away from directly coaching her, I was able to really focus on the details of her game. The game became more fun to her. We talked more about the intricacies of the game, and how she could improve. It was actually more enjoyable for both of us. In releasing "my" players, they both became more skilled, Simply put, their skills reached levels that I would not have been able to get them to. Nerlens received a D1 scholarship to the University of Kentucky. One year later, he was the 6TH overall selection in the 2013 NBA draft.

With Scott Hazelton's training, Jaylen has become a more well-rounded player – which provided the foundation for more advanced skills training through her work with personal basketball trainer Claude Pritchard. After a lot of hard work she began receiving offers and committed to play basketball for Penn State, the summer after her 9TH grade year.

In this section, we will discuss how to develop skills. Camps, weight training, personal coaches and playing other sports, go a long way in helping to develop and improve skills. Additionally, I'll explain how picking the right high school program is imperative to the skill development process.

Remember it is fundamentals and skill development which that allow a slightly above average athlete to perform at an exceptional level.

Camps, Clinics, Personal Coaches & Showcases – *"Caveat Emptor"*

Caveat Emptor is Latin for "Let the buyer beware." Be careful with camps! "Not everything that glitter's is gold." CAMPS ARE NOT the "MAGIC BULLET"! I have seen countless dollars spent by parents on camps, with the hopes of getting their son or daughter to the next level. There is a strategy for camps and you should carefully follow and learn from my successes and failures in the Camp section.

Brennan attended his first football camp when he was about eight years old. He went to my former teammate's (Chris Slade, Patriots Linebacker) camp which was held at a nearby college. It was a shoulder pads and helmet contact camp. The next three summers he attended the "Offense-Defense" full contact camp. Many advise against full contact camps, but I feel that football players need to learn how to hit – THE RIGHT

WAY! So I chose reputable organizations that focused on teaching proper hitting techniques.

Most football camps that are named after a local pro player are run by the same company. They contractually agree to pay the player for the use of his name. For example, the Chris Slade camp, became the Troy Brown Camp, that became the Matt Light Camp, which (at the publishing of this book) is the Devin McCourty Camp. Sports International runs camps in or around every NFL city using the name and likenesses of local football heroes. Again the quality of the camps may vary from city to city but they do have a system and a format that helps to develop player's skills. I have had the opportunity to attend several of their camps as the keynote speaker and found their camps very well run.

Having been exposed to several camps I believe the Football University (FBU) camps are the best teaching camps in the country. Although they can be *pricey,* I have found the training and teaching platform they provide second to none. FBU hires highly qualified coaches to work with the athletes in their nationwide camp series. Former and current NFL coaches, NFL players, college coaches, high school and youth coaches – make up their staff. Furthermore, FBU's parent company is the All American Games (AAG) which runs and selects athletes for the US Army All American Game.

Don't expect your son to get a week's worth of one on one teaching from the "player" who has his name is on the marquee. Some players are more involved than others.

After I gained confidence that Brennan was not afraid of contact, I moved him to non-contact, more skills and technique focused camps. One of my former coaches, Bill Parcells used to say, "if they'll bite when they're puppies, they will bite when they're dogs." That was my approach to camps – teach him how to hit properly, find out if he'd hit, and then focus on techniques.

To be brutally honest, I am not convinced that the camp "system" really works (hence the aforementioned warnings) in developing football players. Most (if not all) camps are run to make money! Teaching the game is probably the third priority, falling behind an enjoyable experience for the campers. As everyone knows, the best customer is a repeat customer who is willing to refer other customers.

Too many camps hire incompetent, inexperienced guys who don't know whether a football is "pumped or stuffed". These guys are usually overseen by a more experienced coach who (depending on the individual) may or may not interact with your son.

Before you send your kid to a camp, get references from respected coaches in the area. Then attend the camp as a spectator to observe how the kids are taught. Locate the camp director, and explain your purpose for attending. Look for college coaches (usually wearing their school colors) that are working with the kids. Look to see if the camp is well organized by getting a copy of the itinerary and monitoring its accuracy. Look for kids wandering around unattended and look at the way the camp deals with injured players. These are just a few areas of which you should take notice. If you see red flags like mistreatment of campers, teaching improper techniques, disorganization, and the like – you should run as fast as you can to another camp.

The myth about camps is that the primary objective is to teach your child the sport. The reality about camps is that they are an opportunity to show what you already know. When players are younger, a good camp will emphasize teaching techniques, but as players grow older and begin to attend camps run by college staffs, the priority is on *scouting* not teaching -- especially at division 1 schools hosting football and (Elite) Basketball camps. These are opportunities to find potential scholarship athletes. But it is also a chance for the college coaching staff to make some extra money. NCAA rules allow coaches to freely interact with prospective athletes who are on (their) campuses. This is a rare chance to get to know a potential player and allow him to become familiar with the coaching staff of the host school.

Youth camps are for fun and teaching. High school level camps are about business and exposure. Camps are expensive and you should be careful not to overdo them. Don't take the high school level camps lightly. These are rare opportunities for your son to show his skills. Make sure he is well conditioned and prepared for the camp! Too many kids go to camps unprepared and out of shape. Camps are usually held in the off-season and players rarely train for them. However, athletes who are serious about these opportunities prepare like the next 40 years of their life depends on it, after all it does.

Every sport has camps and clinics. I have found that camps hosted by colleges are great ways of exposing kids to the college campus. Talk to coaches you respect for advice on camps and clinics to attend. Beyond this, reach out to the camp coordinator, ask for references, and understand the objective of the camp. Simply put, DO YOUR HOMEWORK!

These types of youth and elite sports camps are special opportunities for exposure. Basketball coaches hold camps for the general public during the early summer break from school. They have an open (online) registration and depending on the school may have hundreds of participants attend. Elite camps, on the other hand, are "wink-wink" by invitation. I say "wink-wink" because colleges are NOT allowed to hold "invitation only" camps. The NCAA prohibits schools from holding events exclusive to a select few. The way coaches get around this rule is to send "targeted" camp info to their top prospect list, encouraging them to attend the "Elite" camp. Moreover, the number of participants at the elite camps are significantly fewer than the general camp.

We actually experienced an exception to this usual exclusivity. Jaylen was invited to an elite camp that had almost 300 kids. Clearly not all of these kids were elite athletes. However, the school had two separate gyms and the "elite" kids were in one gym while the other kids were in the other gym. The coaches floated between both gyms to ensure a good experience for both groups; however, they spent a lot more time interacting with the "elite" kids. Remember these camps are recruiting opportunities.

The Penn State Elite Camp had about 50 participants – many were elite prospects – but the majority were (just) good basketball players. Of the 50 kids attending that summer, 3 kids were already committed to PSU, and they extended 2 additional offers. One was to Jaylen. So be careful assuming that a college camp is an automatic way in. I'll say again, only 2 new scholarships were offered to a group of 50 student-athletes.

In addition to college camps, Jaylen attended exposure camps. Unlike football, exposure camps in basketball are heavily attended and scouted by college coaches and scouting services. Make sure you refer to the NCAA Recruiting Calendar to fully understand what is permissible during the dates of any camp or clinic.

Awards Should NOT be the GOAL!

At the well-regarded Chris Slade Camp, Brennan was selected as Best Lineman in the 8 to 10 year old age group. I think he was selected because the coaches were surprised that an 8 year old could hold his own against 10 year old kids. I also think the fact that he was the son of a former New England Patriot made them take notice. Unfortunately a lot of awards are given to kids who really don't deserve acknowledgement. I once worked at one (poorly run) camp that gave out awards based on who had the prettiest mom. Winning awards is great; but try not to have your kid focus on winning awards. The real *reward* is in improving and becoming better at their sport.

Still, working at camps over the years I have learned a few tricks to increase the likelihood of winning an award. So if **awards** are important I would suggest taking the following steps.

1. Use a catchy Nickname – Coaches usually work 5 or 6 camps in a summer; so names and kids may run together. A cool nickname like "Beast", "Showtime", "Jumbo" or "Killa" grabs notice. Throwback names like "Butkus", "Manster" or "Night Train" for football may provoke interest. While in basketball "Magic", "MJ", or "Bird" really get attention.
2. Hustle – Outwork your peers in every drill. Be relentless.
3. Be Respectful – In this day and age, where kids can be "smart-mouths", "yes sir" and "no sir" can go a long way.
4. Wear the same shirt or jersey every day. This makes you easy to remember.

Fortunately over the years, we never resorted to such trickery, but I remember working at a football camp and having a kid nicknamed "MAZ" who did all of the above and for three years straight he received an award -- Best Lineman, Camp Spirit Award, Leadership Award. I always felt he was deserving of something because he was a pretty good player. But when we sat down the night before camp ended, his name was the easiest to remember. He went on to be a pretty good high school player, but (based on his trophy case) you would have thought that he was the second coming of Mean Joe Green.

Most camps will also give an evaluation of your kid's strengths and weaknesses at the end of the program. Take these "evals" with a grain of salt! Most of them are done the night before camp ends, after the coaches have had a few beers – and may or may not be totally accurate. Instead, use these evaluations to reinforce those things you already know about your child. BE REALISTIC! You know your son or daughter has weaknesses; and, if they are exposed or identified by a coach, use this to give your athlete an area for improvement. Use it as a teachable moment. When a coach told me that

Brennan needed to improve his speed and coordination I didn't get upset, because I knew he needed to improve in those areas.

It was very important to my wife and me that we developed well rounded children. When Brennan was 4 years old we signed him up for Karate. Ten years later he became a Black Belt. During the journey to his Black Belt, he improved his speed, flexibility, and coordination. He often jokes that everything I allowed him to do was meant to improve his football skills. Karate – focus, footwork, handwork, flexibility; basketball – footwork, change of direction, jumping, lateral quickness; wrestling – toughness, leverage, conditioning -- he may have a point!

Jaylen on the other hand fell in love with basketball at the age of 4 while playing in the local Y kid's league. We certainly encouraged her to participate in other sports. She played soccer, t-ball, and gymnastics. Again I was accused of picking sports that would help strengthen her athleticism for basketball. The reality is that by encouraging our kids to play other sports, we are in fact helping develop abilities which benefit their achievement in the one sport they choose to focus on.

In no way did we set out to build "football or basketball machines." Looking back, by seeking to develop well-rounded people – music lessons (guitar, piano), playing multiple sports, (Jaylen's) horseback riding, attending art and academic camps, along with involving our children with church and community related organizations – we developed young people who were ready for the rigors of the college recruitment process. Remember, schools are looking for well-rounded individuals, not just athletes.

The emphasis on individual awards, and the misuse and/or misinterpretation of evaluations, are two reasons why I'm NOT a big fan of camps. Often kids will go to these camps, not win an award and come away thinking they're not good players—or, even worse, believing they have no future in the sport. Beyond this, they might get an evaluation put together by a coach who had a "few too many" (worst case scenario) and who couldn't pick your kid out of a police lineup with two people in it. All too often, both the parent and player believe everything positive, or negative as the gospel truth. These are some of the downsides of what can also be a very fruitful development experience.

I have the great fortune of having a wonderful wife who often reminds me that there is another perspective. One year after leaving a football camp I noticed she was VERY upset. When I asked if something was bothering her, she answered "yes." She wanted to know why our younger son Camren, who had participated in the camp, didn't receive an award. I jokingly replied, he must not have been "good enough." My quip was met with an angry "WHAT DO YOU MEAN, HE'S NOT GOOD ENOUGH?" It was at that moment that I looked at camps from the perspective of the mother of a kid who wasn't chosen or acknowledged. Over the years, Camren has won the most athletic awards of all of our three children; but his first camp experience was not viewed as positive by his mother. His camp coach/counselor never introduced himself to my wife, or said what a great job Camren did all week and how it was a pleasure coaching him. Moreover, he never told my wife that her son was "special" and that Camren was going to have a great future in football. It changed my personal approach to camps and parent interaction – forever. Every attendee, player, or "playa" must feel special after he leaves the camp. Although Camren felt proud of his week, his mother felt he had been short-changed. Since that time, I have made it my mission to find something positive to say to every kid I coach. I realize words have power.

To sum it all up, camps can be great tools for teaching proper techniques, improving skills, and learning some specialties for your child's sport, or specific nuances for their position. *But choose camps wisely.* If your son is a "drop-back" pro-style quarterback, don't send him to the *Naval Academy School of Option QB Play.* Find camps that fit your kid's talents and have coaches who can teach him play his position better.

When I was growing up, my mother (single parent) had no clue about what I could handle in regards to football, so she sought the advice of my coaches and others whose opinions she felt she could trust.

Up to this point we have focused on teaching camps. Earlier I mentioned Brennan's acceptance into the Nike Football Training Camp. This is an "elite" camp for players who are individually invited to participate because of selection or recommendation.

In my day (early 80's) there were no such things as combines and elite camps – colleges found players by scouting high school games and discovering talented players among those fortunate enough to attend their own camps. So, when I was confronted with this new era of recruiting through combines and select camps, I had no idea how to navigate this new style approach.

Scouting services like Rivals.com, 247 and Scout.com, among other things, serve two important purposes. They provide information to colleges who are looking for players and they provide information to players who are looking for colleges. One important thing they do is to provide recommendations for elite players to attend select events like the prestigious Nike camp.

When Brennan was in high school, Nike rans about 10 camps a year at select sites around the country. In today's recruiting environment Rivals.com has partnered with Under Armour for their own camp series, looking to identify the top schoolboy players in the country. They invite just 300 to 400 players to each camp. So, simply being invited is a great accomplishment. Brennan attended the Nike Camp held at Penn State in the Spring of his Sophomore year – which was a year earlier than most attendees. In fact, there were only five 10th graders participating at the camp. Many thought it was too risky to send him to the camp, because if he were to perform poorly it could wreck the confidence and the momentum we had worked to build. I viewed it differently. I saw it as a chance for him to compete against really good players and get a "leg up" on the next year's camp competition. I felt as though I was giving him the advantage of competing at the camp when the results didn't matter. Moreover, it would allow us to further identify strengths and weaknesses and better prepare for the next year, when it really counted. I thought it would be beneficial for him to treat the first year as a "dress" rehearsal for following year's real performance.

As I mentioned earlier, he did a great job. Walking off the field he received his first (albeit) unofficial scholarship offer. After returning from the camp, his high school coach's phone was ringing off the hook. Recruiters wanted to find out more about this (then) 6-5 255 pound offensive/defensive lineman.

Of the 119 Division 1 collegiate programs, about 60 were actually represented at the camp. Coaches had a chance to get up close and personal look at all of the prospects. It has been referred to as a "meat market" or "cattle call", because the players are weighed, measured, and herded around from drill to drill to show off their "wares". You'd hear scouts whisper – "too tall, too short, he's fat, bad feet, can't move." It's NO PLACE for the faint of heart, and you should prepare your son for the challenging environment.

In addition to the pressure from hundreds of drooling coaches, I reminded Brennan that there were going to be a lot of players in attendance who would be bigger than he was, stronger than he was, and faster than he was. Still, I told him that no one could measure his heart and desire, and that it was up to him to show it.

As I watched him perform, I thought back to the first day he ran onto the field in Easton. "This kid has come a long way." As proud as I was of him at that moment, that day would pale in comparison to a day we would share 18 months later. Beyond this, as great as those days were – they fall significantly short of the Friday night in April of 2013 when the phone rang with the Houston Texans making him the 89th overall pick in the NFL draft. Needless to say, the journey with your student athlete will be an emotional rollercoaster. As each accomplishment becomes the best yet, do your best to stay in the moment. It becomes very easy to hastily move on to the next goal or objective. From time to time, "stop and smell the roses."

Identifying and assisting the *Next Generation* of great athletes has become a driving passion for me. I noticed an increasingly disturbing trend in youth camps. "Exposure" camps and clinics were popping up everywhere, promising *everything* to youngsters hoping to play their sport at the collegiate level. Recognizing that college coaches are identifying athletes earlier and earlier, exposure camps began to focus on younger athletes. These camps promised prospects training, teaching and (most significantly) exposure to college programs.

In a two year study of these "exposure" camps, I sought to understand their purpose, objective, and most importantly, their success rates. As you've already seen, I have no issue spending resources on trainers, camps and clinics when I genuinely believe it will benefit my kid's recruitment. In this instance, I knew I needed more information.

What I found was did not really surprise me. Most of these camps offered minimal training. The teaching was also inconsistent from camp to camp. Most regrettably, the all-important and extensively-hyped "exposure" benefit was quite often non-existent.

After a year of witnessing these "sham" operations in frustration, I reached out to Mike Farrell of Rivals.com for advice. Mike is referred to as the "Godfather" of college football recruiting. His knowledge of the recruiting process as it relates to football is unsurpassed.

Understanding that Rivals.com had an established and well-regarded process for identifying top high school athletes in place with their Rivals Camp Series, I knew we had a lot in common. We discussed partnering to provide a *truly legitimate* exposure platform for middle school athletes.

In January of 2015, I ran my first NextGen All America Showcase Camp in Boston. A tremendous group of 150 sixth, seventh and eighth grade football players attended the event.

Of that number, 7 were selected to receive profiles in the prestigious Rivals.com Recruiting Database. In our first year of showcase events we entered more than 100 athletes into the NextGen database. More importantly, athletes that attended our events have received nearly 100 scholarship offers. After our second season, more than 300 scholarships have been offered to athletes that have attended our NextGen Camp Series. Our events have garnered so much attention, that the Pro Football Hall of Fame hosted our Top 100 Showcase "THE SHOW".

The event featured the top 6th, 7th, 8th and 9th grader in the country – and was the only football camp covered by all (Rivals, Scout, 247 Sports, ESPN, and Youth1) of the major recruiting services.

Brennan's Camp Chronology

8 Years Old

- Chris Slade Camp

9 Years Old

- Chris Slade Camp

10 Years Old

- Offense Defense Camp

11 Years Old

- Offense Defense Camp

12 Years Old

- Offense Defense Camp

13 Years Old

- Boston College Lineman Skills Camp

14 Years Old

- Boston College Lineman Skills Camp
- Syracuse University Football Camp

15 Years Old

- Boston College Lineman Skills Camp
- Penn State University Football Camp
- New England Elite Football Camp

16 Years Old

- Nike Football Training Camp
- Notre Dame Football Camp
- Boston College Lineman Skill Camp
- Ohio State Football Camp
- University of Virginia Football Camp
- New England Elite Football Camp

17 Years Old

- US Army All-American Combine
- Boston College Football Camp (Unofficial Visit)

Considering that I'm not always a big fan of camps, Brennan sure has been to a lot of them. Although I have reservations, good camps clearly do serve a purpose. As you will notice, my son attended quite a few camps during his sophomore/junior year. This was *the year* when I felt he was ready for national exposure. Again, at the outset of our journey I told you I would share both my successes and my failures. I said would highlight the good things, as well as the (numerous) missteps. With Brennan, my first "project" – the "guinea pig" – I learned that all of the camps we went to not necessary.

What's *the year* (recruitment-wise) for your child's sport? It varies by sport, by region, and by gender. Take time to research your child's sport and recruiting cycle. Understanding the recruiting landscape for your athlete is critical to navigating through this process successfully.

As I mentioned, camps are expensive and you may not have the financial means to take your kid to all of these camps. You may have to be more selective. One of the mistakes I made with Brennan was taking him to exposure camps that didn't provide the exposure we were looking for. Prior to registering for and attending exposure camp, find out which college programs or scouting services will be in attendance.

In Brennan's most strategic camp year, we went to six events. Fortunately they were not all back to back, the Nike Camp was held in May and the others were held in the summer.

Riding the momentum created after the Nike Camp we scheduled several more camps. Each camp was strategically placed. We chose the early session of the Notre Dame Camp, followed by the first session of the BC Camp. Then we went to the Ohio State and Virginia Camps, lastly the New England Elite Camp, a local event attended by his high school team.

We selected the Notre Dame Camp for two reasons. Although they were struggling during Brennan's high school years, Notre Dame is *still* one of the premier college football programs in the country. Beyond this, Notre Dame typically only offers football scholarships to high profile players from all over the country. Thus merely receiving a scholarship offer from the Fighting Irish puts a prospect on the map. Because of their academic standards, an offer from Notre Dame shows that a prospect is also academically viable. I looked at the Notre Dame opportunity as a scholarship "certification". I explained to Brennan that if Notre Dame offered him (a scholarship), that he would probably have his choice of any Division 1 program.

Brennan attended the ND camp with two of his teammates and enjoyed himself at the camp. Interestingly, he didn't like the school or the campus. And, although he performed well at the camp and received a lot of attention – he didn't receive the scholarship offer we were hoping for.

As we boarded our flight home to Boston, we talked about the type of school he would like to attend. He was not able to explain exactly the type of school he wanted to attend, but he knew it wasn't Notre Dame.

Unbeknown to us his trip to Notre Dame had created a buzz, not in South Bend, but back in Boston. As he arrived on the Boston College campus there was a lot of anticipation (from the BC coaches) for his arrival. They knew he was arriving a day after the beginning of the camp because he was in Indiana attending the ND camp. Shortly after arriving at the BC camp, Brennan attended his testing session at the camp. Most camps get heights and measurements and put players through some basic tests, like the 40 yard dash and vertical jumps – to determine if the athlete is a legitimate prospect. With all of the excitement surrounding his arrival, anything more than "falling on his face" would get him a scholarship offer. He measured 6' 5" and weighed in at 260 pounds. He ran a 5.2 (just average) 40 time; but he dominated the camp's "Showcase" drills.

Each year at the BC camp, among the five or six hundred kids in attendance, the BC coaching staff will look for players with exceptional measurables, abilities, and/or talents. These players are pulled aside during the camp and put through drills with other players who also have been selected. BC calls this the **Showcase** – these drills and tests are reserved for the best players in the camp and closely observed by the scouting services and other college coaches in attendance. It's a "big deal" to make the Showcase!

The evening of his second night in the camp, I went over to watch our high school team's skill players compete in a 7 on 7 passing game tournament. I was approached by the offensive line coach Jack Bicknell, who introduced himself to me and wanted me to meet the Head Coach, Jeff "Jags" Jagodzinski. The first words out of Jags' mouth were, *Brennan has a scholarship to Boston College*, and we would love to talk to your family about the possibility of him attending BC. I also thought it was funny that the second thing he said was "what did you think of Notre Dame?" It obviously was a concern.

As a PCM (Remember? "Parent-Coach-Manager"), you really need to know your kid's strength and weaknesses. Early in Brennan's (scouting) camp career I told him not to run the 40 yard dash testing because I didn't feel he would perform well. In the 7th grade Brennan was diagnosed with Osgood-Schlatters disease, a painful knee condition that is very common with adolescent boys. During his 7th and 8th grade years he struggled when running full speed, so much so that he changed the way he ran to offset the pain. This change in running form caused him to run slower; and since there is no cure for Osgood-Schlatters, we had to treat the symptoms and wait for him to outgrow the condition.

After his 8th grade football season, the doctors recommended that he skip the upcoming basketball season. They told him that he could participate in a low impact sport, so he chose to wrestle. The painful condition continued until his sophomore year. During that three year time span I explained to him that running a poor 40 yard dash at a camp could hurt his chances of being recruited. In reality, the 7th, 8th, and 9th grade years were not big deals: however, we didn't want to risk a poor showing *after* his Freshman year. I recognized that his performance in "position specific" drills would bring him positive attention, but felt that a poor 40 time would cast question marks on his athleticism. Moreover, the position drills didn't cause him as much discomfort.

When you send your son or daughter to camps (especially exposure camps), you should recognize that if they struggle in an area because of an injury or lack of development, you are NOT compelled to have them perform the test. Furthermore, if he or she does test poorly, you have the option of requesting that the results be removed from their record. This is important because – long after the camp is over – the coaches will have copies of the camp results, and all they will see are the numbers. If they see a 6' 5", 260 pound sophomore, their interest may be peaked. However, if they see a horrible 6.5 second 40 time they may lose interest. In my daughter's case, if they saw a 6' 3", freshman forward, they'd likely continue monitoring her throughout the showcase season.

Just remember that with camps, **you** are in control!

I am sure you are looking at the list of camps Brennan attended and wondering, "How much money did all of these camps cost?" I realize that a similar camp schedule may not be affordable to everyone, but I'd also suggest that you don't have to take this route. We may have gone overboard with the "camp thing." As I mentioned, my second son. Camren – jokingly (but affectionately) referred to as my *second project*, benefitted from the lessons learned with "Project 1". We adjusted his camp schedule accordingly:

To better detail Camren's schedule, I will use categories to show the camps Camren attended. (They were also attended by Armani Reeves.)

Developmental Camps

- Offense/Defense (2 years)
- Football University (2 years)

Showcase Camps

- Nike Football Training Camp (2 years)
- Rivals 7 on 7 Showcase (2 years)
- NextGen All America Camp*
- Under Armour Camps*
- Adidas Football Showcase Camps*

*New Camps

College Exposure Camps

- Boston College (3 years)
- North Carolina (2 years)
- Connecticut 1 day showcase
- Wake Forest 1 day showcase
- Virginia 1 day showcase
- Michigan State 1 day showcase
- Penn State 1 day showcase

As you will note, Camren's schedule was a lot different than Brennan's. "Project #2" and "Project #2.5" (Armani) required a different approach. Some of the changes were prompted by Brennan's experience – while other revisions were made because Cam and Armani played "skill" positions. Lastly, colleges made the adjustment of adding one day showcases to better accommodate athletes and make the process more affordable.

The one day showcases are great! Since most college camps are held over a two-week period in June, it's really hard for players to attend several camps. Most college camps last 3 or 4 days and having a player participate in the full camp can be risky. Poor performance, injury, and fatigue risks indeed forced me to curtail Brennan's "big" camp year.

Camren and Armani could be exposed to a lot more because of these one day opportunities. In fact, to call the Penn State event a one day camp would be a huge overstatement. We arrived at Penn State at 10 AM, paid the $50 fee required for a one day camper. The boys went on the field at Noon. We met (then) defensive back coach Kermit Buggs and (then) defensive coordinator Tom Bradley for a series of drills. The drills lasted about 20 minutes. They were the only 2 players working out during the session. Armani made a one-handed catch where he appeared to be 12 feet in the air. Coach Bradley responded with an exuberant WOW! Camren demonstrated the ability to cover an elite college wide receiver prospect (Armani). And after about 15 minutes coach Buggs and Bradley gathered the boys and asked if they wanted to get lunch. We (of course) said yes! We arrived at the lunch table to meet their area recruiter, (then) offensive line coach Bill Kenney – expecting him to talk about their participation in the full afternoon session. Instead he offered them scholarships and told them that they didn't need to work out in the afternoon session, rather he would set up a campus tour to allow them to familiarize themselves with the school.

Most parents refer to the money spent on Brennan's football camps as "costs". I choose to call it an investment. In total, I invested about $8,000 in camps for Brennan. However, the value of the college scholarship he received is more than $200,000. In my formal profession as a financial advisor, I would call that a pretty good return! The $8,000 investment sounds daunting, however when you divide it by 10 years it's a more palatable $800 a year. At 6' 6" and nearly 280 pounds, I often joke with Brennan that the weeks he was away at the various camps actually saved our family money because of the reduction in groceries.

As I mentioned at the outset of this book and earlier in this chapter, there are some mistakes I made throughout this process. Camp "overkill" may have been one of them. But remember, due to the obstacles I was facing as a PCM from the lowly regarded football state of Massachusetts, I felt it was important for Brennan to compete outside of the state and prove to himself that he could play with anyone from anywhere.

Basketball (or your kid's competitive sport) is more than likely an entirely different animal. Each sport has its own unique recruiting facets – this includes camps, showcases and recruiting timelines.

Jaylen's camp and showcase journey was nothing like the boy's football experience. This was due largely to the access permitted by the NCAA at college showcase events. Familiarize yourself with the term "LIVE EVENT" – a Live Event is any event or showcase that allows college coaches to attend in-person. Football attendance (D1, D1-AA, & D2) is limited to events held by colleges on a college campus. While in other sports, the NCAA allows coaches to attend non-campus events provided certain parameters are in place.

Jaylen attended several camps when she was a young basketball player. While in elementary and middle school she attended college camps for development and for fun. It is important to state that the NCAA defines a student-athlete as a "PROSPECT" differently depending on the sport. For football it occurs in the 9th grade; however, with most Olympic sports it's much earlier. In basketball, student-athletes become prospects in the summer after their 6th grade academic year. It's important for you to know when your collegiate sport labels your student-athlete as a prospect, because that determines both when and what types of contact are permitted by the NCAA. This is critical because the earlier your sport refers to your kid as a prospect, the sooner the recruiting process begins.

Since the process starts earlier in basketball, Jaylen's camp schedule was much different than her brothers'. Jaylen received an invitation to one of the nation's largest showcase events for girls basketball the summer before her 9th grade year. Every year, the All Star Girls Report (ASGR) Top 10 Camp invites 200 of the top high school basketball prospects in the country to compete in a "Live" showcase event. Most of the girls competing are in their sophomore or junior year, Jaylen was one of just five 8th graders allowed to attend.

There are literally hundreds of showcase camps that refer to themselves as "Elite Camps". However, there are only a few that can garner the attention of college coaches. The ASGR Top 10 Camp, run by Bret McCormick, is one on of them. Bret scouts girls basketball players starting as early as the 4th grade. He covers camps, clinics, tournaments, summer leagues, and high school games—(basically) anywhere girls play ball. His list of prospects is purchased by college coaches and recruiters. ASGR also runs their own tournaments and events – and they do a tremendous job promoting girls basketball.

So when Jaylen was invited to Bret's camp, I jumped at the opportunity to get her there. Since I wasn't as knowledgeable about basketball recruiting, I asked some college coaches for their advice prior to agreeing to attend. One coach told me that the fact that Bret actually knew my daughter's name was big and the fact that he invited her at such an early age was huge! The coach told me that if we were serious about her playing college basketball – we would be "crazy" not to attend.

The ASGR Camp was the only "real" showcase Jaylen attended. The only college camp she attended (as a prospect) was Penn State's. In fact, her entire camp experience was literally comprised of two events. She committed to Penn State the summer after her Freshman year.

My formula for determining good exposure events in basketball is pretty simple: FOLLOW THE SHOES! If Nike,

Adidas, or Under Armour are sponsoring the event – it's probably the (proverbial) **"place to be"**.

The bottom line with camps—consider the "end game". What will your child gain by attending the camp? If the goal is technique, make sure the coaches stress sound fundamentals. If the goal is exposure, ask yourself the question – "Who and what is he (or she) being exposed to?" Lastly, don't underestimate a goal that many fail to see as important, the goal of *having fun.*

Before signing your kid up for a camp make sure you set goals and expectations for attending. At the end of the camp, ask yourself if the objectives were met. Furthermore, ask if the camp exceeded your expectations in any way. If the focus is technique and fundamentals, your son or daughter *should* walk away from the camp having learned something new. It's also key that your kid will be persuaded to practice those techniques until he or she can comfortably use them. If you were looking for exposure, you should know (prior to attending) who the observing scouting services are, as well as, how they evaluate, report and disseminate the information on the player's performances.

If college coaches are allowed to attend, which schools frequent the camp? College coaches are creatures of habit. If they have had success finding talent at a particular event, rest assured they will return. More importantly, (if college coaches can't attend) you need to understand who subscribes to the information generated by the camp. If they are sending the information to Division 3 schools, and your goal is D1 – that's not the camp for you!

As previously discussed, college camps can also offer exposure. Most noteworthy D1 football schools allow coaches from other area schools which compete at the lower D1-AA, D2, or D3 levels to serve as coaches in their camps. The purpose of this access is to offer the opportunity for the smaller programs to scout attendees who don't project as D1 caliber players. Most big programs welcome coaches from smaller ones. These coaches actively look for opportunities to make a little extra money and get a jump on recruiting. During Brennan's recruitment, Ohio State went a step beyond opening the door to (just) D2, and D3 schools. They also invited coaches from "mid-majors", or smaller D1 colleges. Programs like Toledo, Bowling Green, and East Carolina were represented the year that Brennan attended the OSU camp. I asked (then) Head Coach (Jim) Tressel why he would allow potential competitors for recruits to get a first-hand view on "his dime?" He explained that he was confident that a player who had the choice to attend either Ohio State or Toledo would choose the bigger, more prestigious program offered at Ohio State. However, if he chose Toledo, "then he wasn't the player we wanted anyway". I don't believe his statement was meant to demean Toledo's program. He was simply saying that if a prospect would rather play on a smaller stage, he (probably) wasn't the type of player that would be successful in the Ohio State program. I also found it interesting that Notre Dame (during the Charlie Weis era) did not allow any other college level coaches to assist the year Brennan attended. They teach and train high school coaches for their camp and each position group is overseen by a member of the ND staff.

As you look for the right college camps to attend, it is important for you to know who will have access to seeing your kid's performance. Recognizing that there are D2 and D3 schools working the camps can give players the opportunity to showcase their skills directly to programs that may be more suitable for their level of play.

Finally, I really do believe "fun" should be a goal (especially in the early years) of any camp experience. You want your son or daughter to love the game. Some of the camps Brennan attended were like a "big sleepover". He went to camp with a few friends and had a blast living "on his own" in a college dorm. He did all the *silly* things that boys like to do, and that mothers hate to hear about, like staying up past their bedtime, not brushing their teeth for a week, laughing at disgusting bodily sounds (from both ends), etc. Both Camren and Jaylen also loved social side of camps. They enjoyed connecting with others players from different parts of the country. These are events that they will remember for the rest of their lives and they should be enjoyable.

Other Sports

In the Tiger Woods, Williams Sisters, Kobe Bryant era of youth sports, I am very concerned about the increasing youth sports specialization. Parents see the success of Tiger and think that they can do the same thing with their son or daughter. So, at a very early age, they focus their kid on one sport – and don't allow their children to participate in any other sports. They become *specialists* in the 3rd and 4th grades, and to the amazement of their parents, "burn-outs" by the time they're in high school.

Locally, I have witnessed a kid on the verge of burnout. He is an extremely gifted young quarterback – that gained national attention at an early age. Although he plays other sports, he plays or trains for football year around. Two years ago he was well ahead of his peers, but non-stop football training has not increased his lead, rather it has brought him back to the pack. Honestly, he is still skilled, but I don't see the drive and passion – and I attribute it to the kid needing a *break*.

My wife is the "balance" master of our family. She can see things in our kids that I don't see. She can see when they need to get away from the game, or (simply) get away from me.

There are several studies and indeed entire books written on the benefits of "cross-training" through playing different sports. Specializing in one sport may develop the muscles and mechanics for that (particular) sport – but it may also overwork those muscles, tendons and joints, while under-working other muscles, tendons, and joints. This pattern may make your young athlete more susceptible to injuries. Of even more concern is the mental fatigue associated with playing a sport *year-round*, especially at early (pre-teen) ages. Rarely are young athletes able to play a sport all year without reaching some level of physical or mental fatigue. Maybe that's why Tiger and Kobe have been historically regarded as *so special.*

I strongly recommend you allow and even encourage your child to participate in different sports. This should not be difficult with football players. Because of the physically demanding nature of football, you CAN'T play year-round. I know you may argue that the phrase *year-round* is liberally used at both the college and professional levels to describe their programs. Although there may be activities that take place throughout the calendar year – the amount of full contact hitting and drills are held for less than half of that time. The other parts of the year are filled with the training and conditioning necessary to allow the body to withstand the more physical periods of the season.

The skills needed for football can be enhanced by participating in other sports. Obviously track and field helps speed. Basketball helps in a multitude of areas. Wrestling aids in leverage. Karate develops flexibility, focus, hand and foot speed. Baseball improves hand-eye coordination. Even the dreaded "S" (soccer) word can help improve football skills.

As I mentioned earlier in the book, the NCAA recently put a new recruiting rule into place. In essence, they've said that a player can't be a college basketball prospect prior to the 7th grade. This rule is supposed to protect young athletes. In limiting prospects to 7th graders and above –coaches are also disallowed from participating as coaches or scouts at "non-scholastic" (away from their college) camps, recruiting combines, elite camps and the like. There has been a rash of college basketball players who are receiving and accepting scholarship offers as early as 8th grade. The NCAA hopes to curtail such activity by limiting coaches from interacting with younger players unless they are (by rule) on their own college campuses.

My belief is that this rule may have the adverse impact of causing coaches to start attending youth camps featuring 4th,

5th and 6th graders. This would further encourage early competitive specialization and the one sport focus phenomenon. Most of these early offers and early recruitment activity involves basketball and not football, largely because it is easier to identify a unique basketball athlete. I ran an AAU basketball program and had a player who was identified as one of the top players in Massachusetts and was highly-regarded nationally. At the time, Nerlens Noel was 6' 8" Forward/ Center, who was very athletic. He played football, ran track and had been dunking a basketball since the 6th grade. He was been invited to attend college basketball games by Boston College, and nearby Connecticut as a 7th grader. He comes from an athletic family, his older brother Jim was the captain at Boston College, and his other brother Rodman was a starting linebacker for North Carolina State. Nerlens was being bombarded by calls from prep schools, private schools, and other AAU programs. Oops, I forgot to mention that he was only 14 and in the 9th grade – while dealing with these pressures. His Dad is about 6' 5" and his mother is close to 6'. By now you know Nerlens as 6' 11" NBA Lottery Pick with the Philadelphia 76ers, after playing just one year at the University of Kentucky. By comparison, when Brennan was 14 and in 9th grade he was 6' 2" and weighed about 200 pounds. A scout could look at him (Brennan) and tell that he *might* be a scholarship athlete, but there was nothing that was a definitive indicator.

The National Collegiate Scouting Association (NCSA Recruiting Network), a sport scouting and recruitment matching service, has put together the following chart for D1 caliber college football athletes. These are the "target" measurables for high school players taken between their Junior and Senior years. (Similar data for other sports is listed in the appendix.)

DIVISION 1 FOOTBALL IDEAL MEASURABLES

Position	Height	Weight	40	Bench	Squat
QB	6'3"	200	4.6	260	425
RB	6'0"	210	4.5	315	415
WR	6'2"	185	4.5	235	315
TE	6'4"	240	4.7	300	440
OL	6'4"	280	5.1	320	450
DB (S)	6'2"	200	4.6	270	405
DB	6'0"	185	4.5	260	385
LB	6'1"	220	4.6	315	445
DL	6'4"	250	4.8	315	450

Source NCSA Recruiting Network

This chart is the starting point for Division 1 level football recruits. Of course there are exceptions to the rule, as different programs adjust their sights because of their system or style of play. Furthermore, these are the prototype measurables that D1 schools are looking for. I have

included the NCSA recommendations for 1-AA, D2, D3, NAIA and D-4 football programs in the appendix.

As you can see, a football player may be more difficult to project – so the importance of playing other sports is not only for the previously described physical and mental concerns. Your son may also find that he is more gifted in another sport.

Lastly, it is important that we PCM's develop well-rounded individuals and well-rounded athletes. Putting all of your eggs in a one "sport" basket may cost you an opportunity in another sport. Nerlens, for example, loved football. However, there are not too many 6' 8" 175-pound (175 is not a misprint) players in college football. Had he limited his athletic experience to youth football, he would not be in position to garner the attention and accolades he's receiving in basketball. He easily became a D1 basketball player. Furthermore, he'll probably be a better basketball player because of his participation in football and track. I will freely admit that it ultimately became necessary for Nerlens to stop playing football – and focus solely on basketball. However, another pretty good high school basketball player – was also an All-State football player—a guy by the name of Lebron James! I think it worked out "okay" for him.

When high school athletes tell me that they are going to specialize in one sport – I use Lebron's story for rebuttal. As most people knew he was destined for the NBA when he was in 8th grade, but he still played football. There are few who have the special talents of a Lebron James – so if playing multiple sports was good enough for him, don't let your son or daughter blindly buy into the merits of a one-sport mentality!

Here's a (cool) fact. Of the 85 scholarship athletes on Camren's National Championship Ohio State Buckeye team – 75 players played multiple sports (nearly 90%). Urban Meyer has publicly stated that he prefers to recruit multi-sport athletes.

Strength & Speed Training

One of the largest growth businesses is sports-related training for young athletes. There are several national companies and countless regional (local) trainers who are very well educated and skilled at strength and speed conditioning. However, there are a ton of "wannabee" experts who may or may not have the credentials to train young athletes. Some are certified trainers, and some are *just* "certifiable"!

This is an area where you should *proceed with great caution* for a number of reasons. First the cost associated with these services can be exorbitant. I know of families who have spent thousands of dollars training their 8 or 9 year son because they saw a future in athletics. Furthermore, training *young* bodies is a specialized service, largely because of growth and coordination issues, and improper training can do more harm than good. You could subject your athlete to irreparable injuries and end their potential career before it begins.

That being said, Brennan started strength and speed training when he was about 13 years old. At the time I wasn't sure what age he should start training. So I consulted some of my old trainers and strength coaches. I spoke with Dana LeDuc

– St. Louis Rams, Jerry Simmons – Carolina Panthers, John Thomas – Penn State, and Johnny Parker – San Francisco 49ers. I trained under LeDuc in Seattle, Simmons and Parker in New England, and Thomas was my college strength coach at the University of Toledo. All of these men are highly regarded experts in the area of football strength and conditioning, averaging just over 20 years of experience, each. Most importantly, I trusted their advice.

When Brennan was about 12 years old, I spoke with each of them for at least an hour and asked their advice about when I should start a formal training regimen for my son "the future football player". Their responses were quite interesting; but after the interviews I was even more confused. I spoke with four experts (from the same field, mind you) and received FOUR DIFFERENT ANSWERS! One explained that kids in Russia start at age 8, another explained that I should start when I see hair sprouting from areas of his body (that he probably wouldn't let me check), another explained that 13 or 14 was a good age, and another recommended high school age to allow the growth plates to start closing.

Although confused, I was able to pull out **three** commonalities from the interviews.

1. Training MUST be supervised
2. Workouts should focus on calisthenics
3. Focus on Technique – NOT WEIGHT, or SPEED

Training Must be Supervised

If you choose to have your son or daughter start a training program, make sure it is supervised by a certified trainer who specializes in working with *young athletes*. As with Camps, get references, and watch the trainer work out their other clients. Interview them, ask questions like; How do you measure success? Are your programs one sport specific? And, what is your typical training cycle?

Workouts Should Focus on Calisthenics

I know we are always searching for the magic bullet, the machine, the weight-lifting exercise that will catapult our sons into stardom. When starting early, training should not be about lifting machines or mastering the power clean; rather the focus should be on doing good push-ups, sit ups, or pull ups. Working on flexibility is huge, as most of our kids suffer from a common disease I refer to as "Playstation-itis". This *condition* is caused by the countless hours of sitting on the floor with their knees bent playing with their Playstations or XBOX's. Improving flexibility improves speed and reduces the likelihood of injury. Kid's should stretch daily. As a Pop Warner football coach, I was always amazed at the number 8 – 10 year olds who couldn't *simply* touch their toes without bending their knees.

Focus on Technique

The best advice that came from my training conversations was: by starting supervised training early you can really focus on technique. The old adage "boys will be boys" definitely applies when it comes to weight lifting. Boys by nature are competitive. So if they have a friend who bench presses 250 pounds, they will sacrifice technique (risking injury) to match or beat their buddy's top lift. By starting early, you can instill the importance of proper technique, teach respect for the various machines and exercises, and minimize the risk of injury while training.

Although she's very competitive, I found it interesting that my daughter Jaylen didn't succumb to the typical weight room antics of many boys. She was much more teachable, always employed good technique, and didn't (really) care how much weight was on the bar or machine.

By starting Brennan's weight-training at age 13, I accomplished two things. First, he developed sound lifting techniques. Second, he was comfortable and confident in the weight room when he started more "minimally- supervised" lifting with his high school teammates.

76

My theory on strength and speed training is fairly complex. In the financial industry that I work in – financial advisors are bound by the New York Stock Exchange (NYSE) rule 405. Rule 405 simply states, "It is the responsibility of the Financial Advisor to KNOW YOUR CLIENT." The same applies to training – know your ATHLETE! Start with a small regimen (without weights) at home. I started with sit-ups, push-ups, pull-ups, calf raises and squats. To encourage my kids I would give them a "bump up" on their allowance if they completed the routine 4 times a week. As they became more comfortable with their bodies, I introduced them to a very "light" weight routine using high repetitions and focusing on technique. From there we moved to a more formal training program with a (family friend) local certified trainer – Barbara O'Donnell, of Fitness First. Barbara focused on a combination of lifting weights, plus strength and flexibility exercises.

At age 15, Brennan began training with EPS Sports Training Director Brian McDonough. Brian was recommended to me by a former teammate (New England Patriot) Troy Brown. I interviewed Brian and liked his approach to training. Brennan trained with him for well over 3 years. Recognizing that Brennan's future was in football, Brian developed a football specific training program that was also position specific. When Brennan committed to the University of North Carolina, he started doing the program designed by Jeff Connors, UNC Strength and Conditioning Athletic Director. But, he did it under the supervision of Brian until he moved to North Carolina. I love kids who go to the gym and work out on their own. However, if the professional athletes have supervision, shouldn't an 18 year old kid?

Strength & Conditioning Training Schedule	
In-Home Calisthenics	Any Age
Light Weight Training	12-14 years old
Formal Training Regimen	15-18 years old
College Team Training Program	18-22 years old

Remember the *love of the game* portion of this book! Make sure your son or daughter has a love for the game prior to entering the formal training phase, as this is also a potential source of "burnout". Remember to take breaks, take vacations, get away from it all to allow your athlete to keep the fire. **Make it fun!** One of the reasons my kids enjoy training with Brian is that he never knows what's next. He rarely does the basic lifts – rather he puts them through exercises that apply to what they do on the field or court. They push trucks around the parking lot – simulating blocking to build leg strength, the boys flip 350 pound truck tires – simulating the explosive need to fire off the line, they run hurdles, jumps on boxes, and he does a lot of short sprints requiring changing direction. Through Brian (Jaylen) has learned to love boxing, as it is a regular part of his training regimen. I've often said that Brian almost tricks them into shape.

I also found ways of making our at home exercises fun and interesting. In the days before unlimited text messaging, each month my wife and I review our cell phone bill to see which of our children have taken the most advantage of the unlimited text messaging allowed in our family plan. Around the first of the month we gather in the family room and I yell out numbers – "Brennan 1500", "Camren 6000", "Jaylen (my daughter) 300", "Armani (my Godson) 1 - 5,000"! The ooohs, ahhhs, awws, and OH MY GOSHES, ring out around the room. They respond this way because our family rule is to divide the number of messages by 30 (days of the month) and make that the number of push-ups, sit-ups, and/or pull-ups they must do EACH DAY! Armani is going to be REALLY STRONG!

Remember this experiment was done with a "pre-teen" Jaylen. Now that she's a teenager Armani's 15,000 would be a slow week for her. We've actually had to adjust the workouts or she would look like Arnold Schwarzenegger – no offense to Arnold, but I would like to get her married off someday.

As the parent of a female athlete you must be aware of anterior cruciate ligament (acl) injuries – that occur at almost epidemic proportions in women's sports. There are countless studies, and beliefs on why these injuries plague female athletes. But no one has identified the "magic bullet".

During Jaylen's sophomore year she tore her acl while participating at Penn State's elite camp. Sitting just 10 feet away, I watched her perform a move that she had done a thousand times. This time the result would be **drastically** different. She screamed, fell to the floor, clutching her knee. Writhing in pain as the entire gym fell silent.

We learned a lot about Penn State that day. First, we learned that their medical staff is second to none. Secondly, we learned that they are a school of integrity.

The team trainer reached out to the team orthopedic doctor and within minutes he met us at the hospital – on a Saturday evening I might add. Evaluated Jaylen, gave us the dreaded diagnosis.

We learned that PSU was a school that stood by their word. As the scholarship offer that she had happily accepted a year before would be honored. As we prepared for the drive home, Head Coach Coquese Washington – assured us that Jaylen would get past this injury. She also explained that "no matter what" your scholarship is still good." I have to admit, that with all the anxious thoughts running through our minds – those words really calmed us down. Moreover, it set the tone for Jaylen's grueling 10 month rehabilitation. As it allowed her not to worry about losing her scholarship – and fully focus on getting back on the court.

You learn a lot about your kids as they go through adversity. I have (always) referenced Jaylen as the most gifted athlete in our family. But now she had to WORK!

Recovering from and acl injury is a long and hard process. There no way I would have ever wished for this injury, but it changed her for the better. It changed her appreciation for the game, her recognition of her God given talents – which improved her work ethic. During that 1 year rehab we lived by two of my favorite quotes, "Things turn out best for the people

79

who make the best out of the way things turn out". Secondly, "Pray like it's all up to God, but work like it's all up to you".

Supplements, Steriods & HGH

In the microwave, 30-minute sitcom, internet age that we live in, everyone wants what they want RIGHT NOW! We are exposed to advertisements that tell us that we can take a pill that will make us faster, or stronger in a week. No matter how many times experts say "there are no short cuts" – everyone still looks for an easier way. Honestly, who can blame them! Even with the allegations surrounding A-Rod, Bonds, and Clemens – why not take a shot, or a pill that will provide both fortune and fame?

As my family and I arrived in San Antonio to watch Brennan play in the All-American game there was a buzz about this "undersized" lineman from Massachusetts who was dominating the drills and practices. Now Brennan has been called a lot of things in his life, but "undersized", NEVER! At 6' 7" 277 pounds he was considered one of the smaller linemen selected to participate in the prestigious game. He was being compared to (then) Virginia commit and current Washington Redskin, Morgan Moses – 6' 8" 350, Alabama alum and San Diego Charger D.J. Fluker – 6' 7 355. Of the 20 linemen selected for the game, 17 of them weighed more than 300 pounds. By contrast, in 1988 I was the biggest starting defensive linemen for the Patriots at 280 pounds. Brennan wasn't small – these kids were (just) HUGE!

Recognizing that players are getting bigger and bigger naturally – those who are unable to reach these levels are sometimes compelled to cheat. Plain and simple DON'T DO IT! And in the language that would make Mrs. Roth (my 7th grade English teacher) cringe, IT AIN'T WORTH IT!!! In the back of my mind I still hear former NFL great Lyle Alzado, a Pro Bowl defensive lineman, crying out softly from his deathbed "don't do it, don't mess with steroids, look at me! It wasn't worth it." Lyle died at age 43 from an in operable brain tumor that many (including Lyle himself), attributed to his use of steroids and human growth hormones.

I also have a few problems with most supplements. First, most don't do what they say. Secondly, the good supplements are very expensive. Lastly, they are rarely used properly.

Most supplements are products of great marketing and rarely deliver on their promises. Even products endorsed by the pros are often not used by the athlete pitching the product. A good trainer can recommend supplements for your kid's specific needs; but be careful, many trainers are also paid to endorse or sell various products.

The *dietary supplement* business is a multi-billion dollar industry. Purchasing these products can be very costly and is probably not necessary for your athlete's development. The amount you spend on supplements tends to "sneak up" on you. Before you know it, you've spent $400 - $500, and may not have results worthy of your investment.

Most importantly, supplements (even the good ones) are rarely used properly. Most kids will use them as a replacement rather than a supplement. Supplements are designed to enhance a well-balanced diet, training, and rest regimen. You (and your kid) need to realize that there is no vitamin or magic pill that will replace "good old" hard work.

If you choose to use a recommended supplement for your son or daughter, make sure you monitor his use. Some young athletes think that if a little will give them a small edge, then a lot will give them a big edge. And this thinking is not limited to kids – in my **10th year** in the league one of my conditioning coaches recommended that I use the LEGAL supplement Creatine as a way to expedite my rehab program. Creatine is a protein that we get from the meats we eat. However, the Creatine supplement increases the amount of protein without ingesting the calories associated with the meat. Usually in powder form, it is added to water or juice and ingested orally. Some increases in strength have been associated with prescribed Creatine cycles – however, many forget to look at the potential side effects.

The coach recommended that I take two small scoops of Creatine powder dissolved in liquid in the morning and evening. Stupidly, I thought that if two scoops will get me ready to play in two months – four scoops would have me back on the field in a month. Needless to say, within a week I was taking about five scoops twice a day, and not following the hydration instructions the coach vehemently recommended. I was starting to see results after about a week (real or perceived – I really don't know), when I began to notice a lot of mucus forming in my eyes when I would wake up. By the 10th day on my program, I woke up and couldn't open my eyes. My eyes had completely swollen shut. After three or four days off of Creatine and drinking a ton of water, I could finally see clearly again. If I (a 10 year NFL veteran) could succumb to this pressure, how can we expect teenagers to make the right choice?

After literally and figuratively opening my eyes, I learned that my Creatine side effect was rare. Usually the side effects include muscle pulls and tears, leg and joint pain, diarrhea and nausea. Overdoses can cause irreparable kidney and liver damages. In fact, because there is so little information on the potential long term effects of Creatine, the NCAA does not allow college coaches and trainers to offer the supplement to their players. It is NOT illegal for players to purchase Creatine on their own and take the supplement; but the school cannot be associated with its use. Prior to this ban, Penn State University's football program did double blind testing of the supplement and found only a 10% differential increase in strength for players in their first or second year and a mere 5% difference for players in their third or fourth year. More importantly, those players using the supplement suffered more muscle related injuries than those who didn't use Creatine. Penn State has determined that the risks outweighed the rewards.

It's that kind of over-zealous approach to supplements that concerns me. I know that there will be those who will continue to take Creatine, and other supplements. My hope is that if you choose to allow your athlete to use ANY supplement you will educate yourself on both the positive and negative effects of using them. Brian has always told my kids that NOTHING can replace eating right, sleeping right, and working hard.

BEFORE JUMPING ON THE CREATINE BANDWAGON CONSIDER THIS!

After Brennan signed with UNC he received a 500 page training manual from Strength Coach Connors. One of the suggestions for gaining lean muscle was for Brennan to adhere to the heavy squat regimen outlined in the book, and drink chocolate milk. CHOCOLATE MILK! Is that all? What about all of the expensive powders, pills, drinks etc? Nope, just drink MILK!

Picking a High School

I struggled with putting the "Picking a School" advice in the Skills Development section of the book. Finally I decided that if you are reading this book, you must have some confidence that your son or daughter has a possible future in sports. Furthermore, if you recognize this possibility, you also realize that all of your best efforts in preparing your son can be ruined in the wrong high school program.

Football is one of the rare sports where the high school program really matters. In basketball and baseball (college) scouts can find talent in AAU programs. In soccer, lacrosse and volleyball elite club teams are a tremendous resource for finding players. But as the parent of a potential football player, keep in mind that your main outlet of exposure is your son's high school.

For example, if you have worked hard developing a prototypical drop back passing quarterback, your work will be in vain if his high school is a "dive option" running team. He may have the best arm in the country, but if all he uses his arm for is to hand the ball off to a running back, no one may ever know.

Choosing a high school program that fits your son's skills set has a major impact on (further) developing those skills. After all, in the analogy I just used – he needs to practice throwing over and over again to become proficient. And it is in those practices, with proper coaching, that he will have the most opportunities to develop his skills.

As I write this section, I am somewhat concerned that some fanatical parent is going to read my book and go on a quest to find the perfect program for their kid by torturing and interrogating high school coaches all over the area. Please recognize that most high school coaches coach the game out of their love for the sport. The last thing they want to deal with is some nut case telling them to jump through "hoops" in order to have his kid play for their team. The reality is that most high school coaches will recognize an extremely talented player and maximize his or her best attributes for the benefit of the team and program. **Do not** use this book as a license to "bully" your kid's high school coach! Remember, he or she is your partner, and they're the first voice that college coaches will listen to regarding your prospective student-athlete.

Picking a school for Brennan was pretty easy for me and my wife. We live in a small town about 30 minutes south of Boston with a high school that offers a very good academic program. In addition, our small town has had a lot of success in girls basketball, baseball, track, and (of course) soccer. Our three children are all products of the town's elementary (K – 3) and middle (4 – 6) schools. During Brennan's 6th grade school year he asked if we would consider allowing him to attend a private junior high school. We had discussed moving him to another school for grades 9 to 12 and were surprised to hear that he wanted to leave sooner.

Brennan had growing concerns that a few of his older friends from his Pop Warner team, who were already in the junior high, had taken some bad turns and started getting involved in things that he wasn't comfortable with. With that as our motivation we began looking into junior high schools in the area.

Our original plan had been to move Brennan for high school because we were worried about our town's football program. The town's high school plays Division 2B football and there was a constant revolving door for coaches and program direction. Adding to our concerns was the fact that we live in Massachusetts, which is not a highly regarded state for football recruiting. In the 10 years that we had lived in Easton, I only recall one scholarship football player going to the 1-AA University of Massachusetts. With the turmoil in the program and concerns with the level of play, I didn't like the odds of Brennan making it to the next level from Easton.

Our plan was to move him to nearby private school and football power Xaverian Brothers High School. We knew that he would get a great education there and have the opportunity to play Division 1 football. The only problem was that Xaverian didn't have a junior high. They started in the 9th grade. So we literally drove one more exit up the road to Catholic Memorial (CM), which had both a high school and middle school.

In our state kids are not allowed to attend a public school unless they live in that school district. This compelled us to look at private schools. Our objectives were simple, we wanted good academics, with a good football program. Little did we know that setting simple objectives for high school would come in handy when it came time for us to choose a college.

Brennan attended CM's Middle School for both the 7th and 8th grades and we had still planned to move him to Xaverian for high school. However, my wife and I viewed this as a teachable moment. We asked Brennan to choose the high school he wanted to attend with the requirement that he had to give us three reasons for the selection. After visiting Xaverian, he gave us three reasons why he wanted to stay at CM.

1. He had developed friendships at the more diverse CM.
2. He wanted to be a part of re-establishing CM's football program.

3. He really liked the Head football coach and felt he had a plan for Brennan's success.

This was great practice for the decision that he would make 4 years later. So choosing a high school was not a tough task for our family. As for the football component of the equation, it was easy for us because of his position. As a lineman, he could play any one of the five positions. Now, if my son were a quarterback or played running back, I would have had to do a more detailed analysis of the offensive system and players that were in the program.

Former Pittsburgh Steeler Andre Jones' son Tai-ler is a highly recruited Wide Receiver in the 2010 class. During Tai-ler's Sophomore year, he attended a school that featured a potent running attack. Because the running backs were getting more than 40 carries a game his receiving talents were sparingly used. Tai-ler only had 22 catches. Although he had a good Sophomore season, Andre felt it was necessary to move him to a high school that threw the ball more for his Junior season. By doing so, Tai-ler caught 81 passes for more than 1000 yards in his Junior year, and saw his scholarship offers go from five to more than 40 offers.

In addition to position and system issues, another important factor to consider when talking to a coach, is his vision and plans for the program. Make sure that you feel comfortable with his direction and leadership. View the coach as a potential business partner – because if things go well, the two of you will work towards a business transaction that could be worth more than $250,000. You may not agree with every decision he makes, but you have to respect the significant role that he will play in your son's development.

Choosing a high school for Jaylen was a little different. After Camren and Armani followed in Brennan's footsteps to the all-boys Catholic Memorial. We wanted to find a place that was just as special for Jaylen's high school experience.

Unlike the challenges that faced our town's schoolboy football program, our Girls Basketball program was thriving.

They had won 2 state championships leading up to Jaylen's entering high school. Furthermore the program had a great coach, one who had been coaching for nearly 30 years. The program had also successfully placed athletes in college programs.

Jaylen and her best friend (and former AAU teammate) Alana Gilmer had always dreamed of attending the same high school. Alana went to a private school in the area.

As a fan of college recruiting I followed the recruitment of Val Driscoll who went on to attend the University of Michigan. Val attended Archbishop Williams, a private school about 20 minutes from our home.

During Jaylen's Junior high years we attended several basketball games to find a good basketball fit. We focused on schools with strong academics and good basketball programs.

On one of our visits we were watching a pretty high profile local coach who had a really strong team. We had heard great things about his coaching acumen and wanted to view it firsthand. During the game I tend to pay attention to things on the court. Strategies, player's shooting form, techniques and basketball fundamentals. My wife on the other hand, watches things like the coach's interaction with the players. She paid close attention to the coach's sideline demeanor, and his players' body language.

During a timeout in a highly competitive playoff game, the coach of the team that we had come to see, began to yell at and berate his players. Prior to this exchange we had (pretty) much made up our minds that this was the school that Jaylen would attend.

As a former athlete – I have been yelled at, cursed at, and (unfortunately) grabbed and shaken. As a coach, I am not overly sensitive to yelling coaches as I have played for all types. As a coach I have found it necessary to occasionally "yell" with the hopes of motivating my players to play their best. However there is a line – and the coach we were watching CROSSED IT!

During his tirade the coach looked at one of his players and yelled, "YOU STUPID FREAKIN' MORON", "What the HELL is wrong with YOU?" He went on to lambaste two other players on the team. As the timeout ended he yelled a few other things and the players left the bench.

In my mind there were two things wrong with his coaching style. First, I don't think it is EVER appropriate to attack a student-athlete's intelligence. Calling the player a moron, is counter-productive and is not likely to get the results the coach wants. Secondly, I noticed that he never gave any instructions. His tirade was filled with insults and attacks on the players – but he failed to give the girls any strategies to address the game situation that they were in.

As I said my wife pays close attention to these areas of interaction and as he uttered the "STUPID FREAKIN' MORON" phrase, she grabbed her purse and looked at me and said, "She is NOT going THERE, we can leave NOW!"

As we were gathering out things to leave the gym I noticed the other team's coach. Very quiet and mild mannered – he seemed to interact well with his team so we decided to watch the rest of the game behind the other teams bench.

As I turned my attention to back to the court, I noticed this coach's team was fundamentally sound. Their best player (Val) was very good and played with great footwork and great shooting technique.

My wife watched his interaction with the girls. The girls on the bench were fully invested into the game, while the girls on the floor played hard and with very little sideline instruction from the coach.

This told us two things, first the program was disciplined. The girls on the bench were focused on the action on the court. Secondly, his lack of (constant) instruction from the sideline showed a confidence in his team's preparation.

Needless to say, that was the day we decided to send Jaylen to Archbishop Williams. As the recruiting process goes, little things matter. Jaylen thought it was cool that the school had the name WILLIAMS on the front of their jerseys. As a 7th grader, she thought it would be fun to have her last name on the front of her jersey.

You'd think that she'd outgrow these kinds of idiosyncrasies, but she hasn't (lol). After leaving a recruiting visit to Boston College, I asked if she was disappointed that they didn't offer her a scholarship. She said "no, I wouldn't go there anyway". I curiously asked why not, she explained that they are not a Nike school and she had a bad ankle sprain in the shoes that they had a contract with at the time. So in addition to great academics and great basketball, her college choice must also have a "shoe deal" with Nike.   I told you girls are different!

3rd Quarter: The Recruiting Process

Understanding the "Recruiting Cycle" for your son or daughter's sport is paramount. The term Recruiting Cycle refers to the various facets that make the up the collegiate recruiting process. For example, at the typical age/grade when student-athletes are viewed, what is the platform for their talents to be evaluated? What camps, what clinics, and what events provide exposure?

To fully understand the recruiting cycle for your kid's sport takes WORK! You need to research the process, by reading books, scouring the internet, and talking to individuals who have successfully navigated through the process.

Understanding what schools are looking for at each competition level is also be included in the cycle of recruiting. I have heard countless people tell me that their kid is a "sure-fire" Division 1 athlete because he or she dominates their high school league, or is a great club or AAU player. Then, upon further examination, it's clear that their kid is not a D1 athlete, and may not (even) be a D2 level player. Homework in this area is critical.

NCSA Sports Recruiting Network offers a "ton" of **free** content that can get you started in the right direction. The website ncsasports.org offers insight into what colleges are looking for at every level, in every sport. Heights, weights, times, points per game, goals, batting averages – you name it, it's there. There are several companies that provide this information; however, this was the site I used, almost religiously.

As Brennan entered 10th grade, his high school coach felt he was ready for Varsity level football. By this point Brennan had been to several camps, played years of Pop Warner football, one year on the Freshman team (8th grade), and one year on the Junior Varsity squad (9th grade). The coach hoped that he would be able to contribute significantly during his first year on Varsity.

All of the camps, and years of preparation were about to pay off. It didn't take long for Brennan to make an impression on the varsity coaching staff. He was inserted into the starting line up on the second day of full pads practice and would be a starter for the next three years.

In football it is important for you to understand that no matter how successful your son is at lower levels, or how many awards and accolades he receives from camps, he *has to* be productive on his high school team. Compared basketball and baseball, where the Amateur Athletic Union (AAU) is available, and soccer, where *club teams* provide the bulk of exposure for college recruiters – high school football is **the** stage that your son must perform on in order to reach the next level.

Jaylen made her high school varsity basketball program as a freshman. She was one of only two freshman that made the varsity team that year. Prior to playing a varsity game she had already received interest from Division 1 colleges. Colleges knew who she was because of her AAU exposure.

Because high school football participation is the primary stage where you have significant choice or control in your kid's ongoing recruitment situation, I stress the importance of picking a good high school program. This is imperative is because your kid's future may depend on it. All of the camps in the world won't open the door to the next level if your athlete doesn't play and play **exceptionally** well in high school. Rarely, if ever, does a college scholarship football player come from any other circumstance.

Picking a good high school for other sports like basketball, soccer, lacrosse, or even baseball is important too. However, because of the other available venues for exposure – picking the right high school program isn't as critical in these pursuits. In fact, Jaylen's high school plays at a Division 3 level in our state. We chose the school more because it was a great academic fit, and because we had great respect for Coach Jim Bancroft and the tradition of the school's program. He had developed several college basketball players, and most recently sent the All-State player Val Driscoll to Michigan. Jim demands excellence from his players and plays THE toughest schedule in the state. Despite being a Division 3 program, they travel to New York, Connecticut and play the toughest teams (at any level) in Massachusetts. If you have the ability to choose – pick a school that looks to challenge your student-athlete.

Back to my football playing boys for a second...understanding the way this high school background thing works, I can tell you that Brennan actually received his first scholarship (verbal) offer at the Nike Football Training Camp held at Penn State. It was the Spring after his first season on the Varsity squad. Though admittedly early, Syracuse University was impressed enough by his performance at the camp to extend a verbal offer. I stress the word verbal, because I am sure if they had researched (Brennan) and found that he was a back-up on his high school team at the time and not yet a very good player in that program, the offer would have mysteriously vanished. Furthermore, when the camp was over, and the list of coaches requesting film was growing, if his high school highlight reel was not at all impressive, the recruiting would have stopped before it got started.

Jaylen on the other hand received her first Division 1 offer while playing for her high school team. As mentioned before, Jaylen was one of two freshman to make a varsity squad dominated by seniors. She averaged 2.3 points per game, 6 rebounds, and 2 block shots. However she averaged 10, 12 and 4 respectively on her AAU team. Yet none of these stats came into play when Providence College offered her a scholarship.

They saw her play a game in New York against a high profile team—a game where she played all of 6 minutes, scoring 2 points with a few rebounds. When I asked the coach what he saw that warranted a scholarship offer in those 6 minutes of action, he smiled and said "nothing". He went on to say "I offered her from what I saw in the pre-game warm ups. She was tall, long, and athletic. She has good shooting form, and on her pre-game layups she tapped the backboard". Then he said, "I looked at my assistant coach and said, 'WOW', we have to get on her *early*."

Both Brennan's and Jaylen's recruiting were somewhat atypical. Usually in football the recruiting process begins with your son receiving a letter requesting information in the form of a questionnaire. Since your address is not public, colleges usually send these initial letters to your son's high school. These initial contacts can bring a lot of excitement. It's important for you and your family to remember this excitement – because as the process goes on, mail *can* become annoying if you don't manage it properly.

If you or your son's school is not familiar with the recruiting process, you may confuse these initial letters and questionnaires with being recruited. Unfortunately, this is just the initial stage of recruiting and simply a process that allows colleges to gather the information so that your son *can potentially be* recruited.

As you can imagine, when Brennan received his first questionnaire we were really excited. Even though he had received an offer from Syracuse, this letter was in "writing" and *must* have meant that this school was going to offer him a scholarship too. The school requested that we complete the questionnaire and send film. We made copies of the questionnaire and practiced filling it out, before completing the official form. *Ignoring the* **FREE** *pre-addressed return envelope*, we then put his highlight film along with the questionnaire into a Federal Express Package and sent it back – marked "PRIORITY OVERNIGHT", please deliver before 9 AM. Talk about OVERKILL! If I had done this for every school that requested information, we would have gone broke!

After reading Joe Hornback's book *The Next Level: A Prep's Guide to College Recruiting*, I learned how to streamline the process. We put together the following bio, since most schools ask for the same information. This bio does two things, first, it gives the school all of the information they request in their questionnaire; second, it shows that your son is probably in high demand because he was unable to fill out their form personally.

93

I felt that the second conclusion reeked of arrogance so we completed the questionnaire *and* included the bio.   In Hornback's book, he suggests you staple the Athletic Resume to the inquiring college's questionnaire and return it. I added a little twist to his advice. Notice the area that says scholarship offers or schools interested in – I would always put (as Joe suggests) inquiring school first on the list. My twist was always to put two other types of schools on the list: one of the requesting school's big rivals, and one nationally recognized program.

Home Contact Information
Home Address   HOME PHONE
Hometown   MAIN CONTACT PERSON'S CELL
                                                 EMAIL ADDRESS

FAMILY
Parents: Brent & Jacquie Williams
Siblings: Brother – Camren – 14, Sister Jaylen – 11

Brent Williams   Jacquie Williams
University of Toledo   Stonehill College
Vice President/ UBS Financial   Model/ Copley 7 Models & Talent
WORK NUMBER   CELL NUMBER
NFL 1986-96 Patriots, Seahawks, Jets

Religion: Christian

2006 PICTURE

ACADEMIC
Catholic Memorial High School   (617) 469-8000
235 Baker Street   Principal: Robert Chisholm
W. Roxbury, MA 02131   Counselor: William Hanson
                                     Coach: Alex Campea COACH'S HOME NUMBER

GPA: 3.25/4.00 Honors/ College Preparatory Curriculum
CORE GPA: 2.75
SAT: 1500
CLEARINGHOUSE: Registered Fall 2007 – 38 Quality Points (15 Classes Completed/In Progress)
                Clearing House ID Number: RECEIVED FROM NCAA CLEARINGHOUSE

College Academic Interest: Computer Studies

ATHLETIC
Height: 6' 6"   Weight: 271   Offensive Positions Played: **OT**, **OC**, OG
Sleeve: 38"   Neck: 19"   Defensive Positions Played: **DT**, DE

40 Yard: 4.95 (6/2008)*   Bench Press: 300 (6/2008)** Leg Press: 875 (6/2008)**
*Tested at Boston College Football Camp   **Tested at Catholic Memorial High School

Other Sports Played: Basketball

SCHOLARSHIP OFFERS: Boston College, Duke, Connecticut, Florida, Maryland, Michigan, Michigan State, North Carolina, NC State, Penn State, Rutgers, Stanford, Syracuse, Virginia & Wake Forest

HOBBIES & INTERESTS: Black Belt in Tae Kwon Do Karate; Computer Art, Weight Lifting, & Paint Ball

COMMUNITY: Member of Jubilee Christian Church Youth Ministry, Member of Catholic Memorial's Leadership & Development Program – Lead Organizer for the Walk for Breast Cancer Fundraiser

Honors: Accepted an Invitation to Play in the 2009 US Army All-American Game, Invited to Participate in the 2009 Under Armour All-American Game. Rivals 250, ESPN 150, 2007 Honors: Most Valuable Junior, 1ST Team All-Catholic Conference, Massachusetts Elite 26, Scout.com Top 100, 2008 US Army Combine Top 50, Rivals US Army Combine 2nd Team DL, 2007 Nike Football Training Camp Invitee.

What I am looking for in a college: I am looking for a school will offer me an excellent education in my area of academic interest. Furthermore, provide an opportunity to play football at a top level in a program that will provide the coaching and training to help me reach the next level.

By listing their program first you show respect for their interest in your student-athlete. By listing the rival school you show that they have competition from a big (familiar) competitor. Lastly, a highly regarded national program gives legitimacy to your kid's credentials. Be careful! DON'T LIE! Don't lie about interest that doesn't exist. The college coaching community is very small, and you don't want to compromise your integrity to expedite the process. Lastly, if at all possible, print the bio in color!

We received early interest during Brennan's junior year. He received questionnaires from a lot of big programs. As I mentioned, we sent his film to 20 different D1 programs and we heard back from 16. One of the schools that responded was Ohio State, one of the schools that did not respond (much to my dismay) was Michigan. Michigan never responded to our prompts; but they did respond when Brennan was listed on the Rivals.com website listing interest from Ohio State and Notre Dame, two of Michigan's biggest rivals. Shortly after the website posted the article, his high school coach received letters from Michigan requesting information.

Ohio State soon stopped recruiting Brennan, but he moved up the Michigan recruiting board and became one of their priority recruits. If we had lied to Michigan about Notre Dame's or Ohio State's interest, we could have cost him scholarship offers from not only Michigan, but Notre Dame and Ohio State as well.

On the eve of the U.S. Army All-American Game in San Antonio, Texas, my wife and I began to reflect. We knew that Brennan was going to make his announcement and verbally commit to the University of North Carolina the next day – and we talked about the long road our family had travelled. If someone had said at the outset of this experience that my son would be a Carolina Tar Heel, I would have thought they were crazy. Over the two-year "serious" phase of recruitment, I would have expected him to select Michigan, Penn State, Virginia, Wake Forest, Notre Dame, Boston College or Rutgers, all of which had been considered a favorite at some point during the process. However, as the recruitment went on, and as we took our time to fully evaluate each school, programs began to disqualify themselves. Not for anything intentionally done in error, but simply based on the criteria and factors we had listed as important to our family.

We put together a spreadsheet with 20 factors that we felt were important to Brennan and our family. We weighted the items and gave each a score from 1 to 10. We were desperately trying to find a way to distinguish between the 15 or 20 schools that were high on our list. To be honest they were all great schools, but we wanted to find the best fit.

We set deadlines for Brennan to move from 20 to 15 schools, 15 to 10 and 10 to five. On June 1, 2007 (the summer of his Senior year) I asked him for his final five. There were actually six including Boston College, Duke, Maryland, Michigan, Virginia, and Wake Forest. We felt it would be impossible to get to know 20 schools, *intimately,* but that it would be a lot easier to educate ourselves on five or six programs. Although we narrowed our list to these schools we remained open to others that fit our academic/ athletic criteria.

During our summer vacation we received two key calls. One from the U.S. Army All-American Bowl Selection committee to inform us that Brennan had been selected, as one of the top 90 players in the country, to participate in the 2009 All-American game. We were thrilled! At this point we'd become less concerned about the opportunity for him to play Division 1 college football. Now our focus was on finding the right college fit for him. In the midst of the All-American game excitement, I received a very different call from the father of a player who was an opponent during Brennan's Junior season.

Tim Adams, the father of Josh Adams from Cambridge, MA, contacted me. Josh was the first football prospect to commit to North Carolina's class of 2009. He was a highly rated wide receiver and his dad and I had met to share recruiting stories and experiences earlier in the recruiting cycle.

Nationally ranked players from Massachusetts are rare, however in 2009 we had 5.

I originally reached out to Tim because I wanted to create a line of communication among the parents of the area's highly rated recruits, so that we could help each other.

Having his son's recruiting "hay in the barn," Tim asked if we had made our final choice, I explained that we weren't even close – and that we had just narrowed the possibilities to six schools. He asked if I would call North Carolina to talk about the possibility of Brennan visiting. As you will learn, during the summer months the recruiting dialogue is reduced because coaches are NOT allowed to call players. The NCAA regulates the amount of contact allowed from coaches to players. If they didn't, as you could imagine, calls would never cease. Because of all of the "hoopla" around the All-American game selection I didn't immediately honor Tim's request.

During the long drive from Florida back to Massachusetts, we had scheduled practice visits at Wake Forest (in North Carolina) and Virginia. On the first leg of the drive I remembered Tim's request, so I called the recruiting department at UNC and introduced myself. I felt pretty awkward, after all *"my boy was being recruited by everyone, and if they wanted him, they should call me."* But the reality was they couldn't contact me because it would have been an NCAA violation. During the call I explained that we were on a pretty tight schedule and would not be able to stop by, but I asked them to keep in touch and maybe we'd visit another time.

Visits: Is it Official?

There are two types of recruiting visits, Official and Unofficial. Who pays? That's the question you need to answer to determine if the visit is official or unofficial. So, whoever utters the phrase, "Check Please", will determine if the visit is official or unofficial. If a school representative says it, consider the visit official or you risk violating NCAA rules.

During our visits to both Wake and Virginia we ate lunch and dinner with the team in their respective cafeterias. At the end of the visits, we received a bill for the food we had eaten. This is not limited to food – as during one visit to UVA we were given (really nice) football jackets to wear while watching practice that was held on a cold December night. As we left the field the coach took the jackets and joked with Brennan that he "knew what it would take to get one of those jackets," he also joked with me "all he has to do is sign with Virginia, but you still have to buy one."

The NCAA allows student-athletes up to 5 Official Visits and there is no limit on Unofficial trips. The best way to know the difference is who pays for the trip. If you pay for the trip it's unofficial. However, if the school pays or reimburses you for **any** part of the trip it's an official visit, and must be reported to the NCAA as one of the five allowable visits. Remember, the school is only allowed to pay for *your kid's* travel expenses. In addition, they are allowed to pay for two parent's meals and hotel costs.

During Brennan's recruitment, here's a trick I learned: If you choose to fly with your son, the school can only pay your son's flight. However, if you drive, the school can reimburse you for mileage to and from their campus. Because this was a family decision for us, we all attended his visits. New recruiting rules allow for the travel expenses of 1 parent/guardian to also be covered by the school.

Brennan made Unofficial visits to several schools. Altogether he probably made 20 or so. Some schools we visited multiple times. We used the unofficial visits because we didn't want to waste an official visit on a school that he had no intentions of attending. Official visits are valuable to both the prospect and the school. As previously stated, players are allowed 5 trips, while schools are permitted to host 56 players during the official visit calendar. In football, the Official visit season begins September 1st of the prospect's Senior season and ends on National Signing Day which is the first Wednesday in February. Actually the visit season is extended to April if a player has not signed. For basketball the visit season starts in April of the athlete's junior year and extends through the late signing period, which is after the Spring of their senior year. Since you only have 5 visits, you don't want use them frivolously. Since schools only have 56 opportunities to host prospects (considering the usual 25 scholarships), if your son or daughter is invited for an official visit, you can safely assume that they are pretty serious about your kid as a prospect.

Am I Being Recruited?

When you receive the first questionnaire or letter, you and your athlete will probably be very excited. I've heard countless players and even parents say that they are being recruited by a school that merely sent them an introduction letter. I hear parents say, Notre Dame is recruiting my son because they received an invitation to the ND Football Camp. Or UConn is recruiting my daughter, because they received an intro letter or camp invite. Of course they want your son or daughter to come to their camp, *because athletes all have to pay to attend.*

While attending a parent's informational seminar at the U.S. All-American Combine, I learned what real recruiting is. The speaker, former (Notre Dame and Michigan coach) Bob Chimel, explained how to determine which mail we received was sincere recruiting interest. Prior to that meeting, I used to say that Brennan was being recruited by about 60 schools. After the presentation I went home and read the mail from each school and determined that there were only 30 schools showing legitimate interest.

Through my additional experiences, I have come up with an easier way to determine if you kid is being recruited. It's just two words— INFORMATION and RELATIONSHIP. When schools are sending your son or daughter information, your kid is merely a name on a list. However "real" recruiting is a relationship business. When coaches seek to develop a relationship with your student-athlete, *then* they *are* being recruited.

100

During Brennan's recruiting process, you knew schools were sincerely interested when you started receiving hand-written personal letters. You will also know that they are sincere in offering your kid a scholarship when you receive a WRITTEN offer from a school. Furthermore, you will know that you are being recruited when coaches contact your school to request your transcripts or check your Eligibility Center Registration (This will be explained in the next segment).

Today coaches hire interns and coaching assistants to send out hand-written notes. The best way to determine whether or not you are being recruited is to see when the school moves from what I call "The Information Stage to The Relationship Stage." Initially schools send out information on their school and program. However as the process "heats up" coaches look to develop relationships with prospects. Social media has become a great way of developing relationships between athletes and coaches.

Because Camren and Armani also attended many of the school visits with Brennan – they were relatively well-known early during their own recruitments. It was tough to decipher the Relationship Stage because they knew most of the staffs through Brennan's recruitment. We quickly learned that they already had relationships. So with them, the indicator that we looked for was the verbal offer. There were a lot of schools that were recruiting Camren and Armani – but they would not extend a "Verbal Offer". Yet soon after they received their first real offer from the University of Connecticut – other schools began to "say the magic words" – "We would like to offer you a scholarship!"

Brennan received about 25 written offers and another six or seven verbal offers. You should know that neither *written* nor *verbal* offers are contractual obligations for a scholarship. In any given year a Division 1 football program may only have 20 – 25 scholarships available to give, but they may extend as many as 50 – 60 offers, some or all of which may be in writing. They realize that all of the players they've offered will not choose to attend their school. But you should *be aware* that some schools are notorious for over-offering. They may offer

100 scholarships with only 20 scholarships available. Additionally, schools also over-accept or "over-sign". By that I mean they may sign more scholarships than they have available. This may or may not be an issue because the school may have players who have decided to graduate. They may have also offered and signed players who won't qualify. There can be a lot reasons why a school with only 15 available scholarships available signs 20 prospects.

Note that football websites like Rivals.com, ESPN, 247 Sports, and Scout.com (unofficially) list the number of scholarships offered by each school. They also list the players and positions each school is recruiting. These sites are pretty accurate; however, they may not be 100% correct. Still, they provide decent estimates.

If you are involved with a school that has offered your son, but has offered more scholarships than they appear to have available – ask the big question! Ask if you kid's scholarship offer is "bound"? The new phrase in football recruitment is "COMMITTABLE OFFER". Meaning, a school offers a kid a scholarship and they are willing to accept the athlete's COMMITMENT right away. A non-committable offer, means that the school has offered an athlete a scholarship on a contingency basis. If they don't get the recruit they want they will convert your kid's offer to a committable offer. **Don't be shy, ASK these questions! Is the offer committable? How much time do we have to decide? Will you notify us prior to the offer being rescinded?**

Specifically for football, ask what the school's plan is for addressing the over-signees? In addition to all of these stated concerns, the school may also plan to have some of their signees enter school early. Some signees may project as "Gray Shirts" (entering later in the process year). Some (prospects) may be projected as non-qualifiers. PROTECT YOURSELF BY DOING THE MATH!

Early signees enter school in January, and actually count towards the previous year's class. Early entrants are usually limited to Fall sports. Gray Shirts are players who defer their enrollment until the following January and can count towards the next year's recruiting class. The other option is a little more complex – schools will agree to sign a player who they know won't meet the NCAA's academic requirement (see sliding scale in the Eligibility Center section) – these players are called Non-Qualifiers. The school signs them and sometimes works to help place them into a prep school, with the hopes of the player returning (having qualified) the next year. In reality, the Letter of Intent signed by a non-qualifier is worthless, because after the player completes the year of prep school he is free to attend any school who offers him. The sponsoring school is not allowed to force the player to attend their university. However, as you can imagine, most of the time players do attend the school who coordinated the prep school opportunity.

I focus a lot of the attention in this book on football recruiting – not only because I have had more experience in football. The reality is that in a high percentage of colleges, football is the sport that pays the bills for the other sports. There are 85 football scholarships versus 15 in basketball, and 20 or so in soccer, baseball and lacrosse. Still, many of the same principals apply.

Jaylen chose Penn State for many of the same reasons that her brothers selected their respective schools. Although many of the same rules and principals are the same, basketball recruiting is a lot different than football recruiting. First, because of the number of scholarships awarded: 85 vs. 15. The number of scholarships per year is significantly less. Penn State is looking to fill just 4 roster spots from Jaylen's 2015 class. They are very specific, they would like to get two forwards, one wing/guard, and one point guard. By contrast, an average annual football recruiting effort looks to fill 25 spots, which is about one player at each position, 11 offensive players, 11 defensive players and 3 others. Most schools use this "formula" as a starting point and tweak the numbers according to attrition.

As for your child's sport, I'll remind you that the smaller the roster, the more selective the recruitment. Another difference in the smaller roster sports is the probability of a more intimate and personal recruiting.

Always remember, the scholarship is not a "done deal" until the deal is done. Exclusively verbal offers can be and are often rescinded. Depending on the school and the integrity of the coaches and administrators – a scholarship can be pulled anytime between when the signing period begins and ends. Most attribute these highly questionable scholarship withdrawals to high profile programs, in big money sports like football or men's basketball. However, a high school teammate of my daughter had her scholarship pulled because the school she planned to attend worried that she wasn't fully recovered from an off-season injury. Sadly she had committed to the school in the Spring of her junior year after suffering a minor knee injury. The school was well aware of the injury prior to accepting her commitment, but chose to wait until a week before the final signing period (more than a year later) to rescind the offer. Completely blindsided, she struggled to find another school to attend. Unfortunately most of the schools who had expressed interest in her had moved on to the next player on the recruiting list.

I would certainly question the integrity of the coach and the school administrators for allowing this action to take place. Still, the example emphasizes my assertion that as a PCM, you've got to do all you can to know the type of program that you are considering.

The NCAA Eligibility Center

The NCAA Eligibility Center is the judge, jury and executioner, as it relates to college eligibility.   The NCAA Eligibility Center is also referred to as the NCAA Clearinghouse. No one gets to D1 or D2 college football without passing the

NCAA Eligibility Center. The Eligibility Center is the division of the NCAA that reviews a players high school transcript, SAT (or ACT) scores, and amateur status to determine if they qualify for college football.

One of my greatest worries as an athletic advisor, coach and parent is the possibility that I could have an athlete who has the skills to play at the next level, but fails to meet the requirements of the Eligibility Center missing out on $200K. The $200K I am referring to is the approximate value attributed to a college scholarship. That number is an estimated amount; however, two of the schools Brennan considered, Duke and Stanford, cost about $55K per year. So based on a five year matriculation (including a Red shirt period) a prospect deemed ineligible could potentially be forfeiting $275K.

No matter what sport your student-athlete plays, these numbers apply. Moreover, this is a critical area of focus and should not be taken lightly, or for granted. The Eligibility Center calculates the grade point average (GPA) of a prospect's CORE classes. Prospective Division 1 college athletes are required to take 16 Core Classes. Newly implemented rules have moved Division 2 requirements from 14 to 16 courses. Although the total number of courses are the same please take notice of the requirements for each subject.

Core classes are **loosely** defined as the following:

	D1	**D2**
English	4 Years	3 Years
Math	3 Years	2 Years
Natural/Physical Science	2 Years	2 Years
Social Science	2 Years	2 Years
Additional (English/Math or Science)	1 Year	3 Years
Additional Core Courses	4 Years	4 Years
Total Core Courses	**16 Courses**	**16 Courses**

The emphasis is placed on *loosely*, because not all math classes, not all science classes, not all English class or social studies courses count. It is YOUR responsibility to log on to the Eligibility Center site (eligiblitycenter.org) and check YOUR student-athlete's school's **specific** qualifying Core Courses. Each school is required to submit course descriptions to the NCAA to allow the governing board to determine if the classes fulfill the core courses requirement. Just remember, that a math class may qualify at one school and the class with the same title at another school may not qualify. One of the kids I advised a few years ago was enrolled in a course titled College Math 1, which looks, sounds, (heck) even smells like a course that should qualify as college preparatory core course. But after checking the **approved course** listing, we found that it did not count as a core requirement. Unfortunately for this young man, it was his Senior year and it cost him a D1 scholarship. He fell 1 course shy of the 16 courses needed. Fortunately for him, in 2008, 1-AA football programs allowed student-athletes to qualify for a scholarship with reduced core class requirements.

In 2007, the NCAA raised the requirements for D1 players from 14 Core classes to 16 Core classes. At first glance this seems like a minor adjustment and change in the requirements. Actually this was a **huge** change! If you notice you from the above course count list you need 4 English classes. Normally students take English 9, English 10, English 11, and English 12. However, If your son or daughter is unable to place into English 9 because their school feels they may not be academically ready, he/she will be behind the eligibility "eight ball". "Remedial" courses don't count as Core. Thus your kid will have to take two English classes at some point during high school. And for a kid who obviously struggles with English, it may be tremendously challenging to take two English classes in the same year. This subtle shift forces parents to not only think about what high school courses their student-athletes must take, but also compels them to be aware of what courses are taken in junior high. Prior to 2015, Division 1-AA and D2 schools were viewed as safety nets for kids who couldn't qualify for scholarship eligibility with 16 core courses, because these programs only required 14. With recent NCAA rule changes, that safety net no longer exists. In order to be eligible for an athletic scholarship a student MUST take (and pass) 16 core courses.

As a parent, I strongly suggest that you meet with your child's 8th grade counselor and explain that he or she is a potential college athlete and you would like to make sure that they are on track to meet the requirements of the NCAA Eligibility Center. I know you are thinking "I am going to sound like some crazy overzealous parent." But, which would you rather be, "the overzealous parent of an 8th grader," or "the disappointed parent of a high school senior who fell one class short of scholarship eligibility?" The former may cost you some embarrassment, while the latter may cost you $250 grand.

To play D1 football, the prospect must pass the Eligibility Center by fulfilling three conditions. 1. A prospective student-athlete has to be a qualified amateur – meaning that he has not accepted payment for play or participation. He is not allowed to hire an agent or to use his football skills to make money. This is usually a pretty easy "hoop" to jump through. The second and third areas are a combination of your son's GPA and his SAT/ACT score. The NCAA uses a sliding scale – meaning the higher the GPA, the lower the SAT/ACT score requirement. Please review the sliding scale.   *SEE   APPENDIX   -   NCAA SLIDING SCALE

Currently there is no sliding scale for D2. Therefore, prospective D2 players are required to have a 2.0 CORE GPA and score a minimum of 820 on the SAT and a sum score of 68 on the ACT. If you student-athlete graduates after August of 2018 he or she will need a 2.2 CORE GPA. A sliding scale will also be implemented during that year.

The NCAA has also adjusted the D1 eligibility requirements going forward. If an athlete has a GPA between 2.0 and 2.3 and meets the sliding scale SAT or ACT test scores, the athlete qualifies for a scholarship – BUT must redshirt their freshman year. A school must be willing to give a scholarship to an athlete that will not be eligible to play their freshman year.

Remember that Eligibility Center requirements only make you *eligible* to receive a D1 scholarship or the D2 equivalent. Some schools have more stringent requirements for admission. A school can raise the NCAA's bar, but they are not allowed to reduce the requirements. For example, schools like Stanford, Notre Dame, and Duke require prospects to meet higher standards for admission than those outlined by the Eligibility Center.

To my amazement, there are three different academic "hurdles" a typical high school student must clear to be eligible for a college scholarship. First you must pass your high school graduation requirements. Second, some states require students to pass a high school competency test. Lastly, the NCAA Eligibility Center standards must be met.

All of our kids attended private Catholic schools in which 4 years of Theology and 1 semester of Community Service are a part of the school's graduation requirements. Neither Theology nor Community service fulfill the NCAA Eligibility Center's core requirements. Yet, in order to graduate our kids had to fulfill the school's credit and course requisites.

The State of Massachusetts requires all students to pass a general competency test in order to graduate from high school. And then there is the Eligibility Center "hurdle".

Make sure your kid is on pace to meet each one of the graduation requirements.

SAT/ ACT Testing

Although some of the top colleges in the country are moving away from using standardized test scores like the SAT and ACT as a part of their admissions requirements, the NCAA still requires that prospective student-athletes take the test in order to be eligible for an athletic scholarship. Earlier we discussed the importance of knowing what position your son should play in order for him to have success on the field. It is also important that you know your son's strengths and weaknesses academically, especially in this critical area of standardized tests.

I have seen, known, or heard about countless prospective scholarship athletes who are unable to get over this critical hurdle. One of the things I watch closely is the number of highly rated prospects who go unsigned after National Signing Day (NSD). For football, NSD is the first Wednesday in February; and is the first day that high school football players can sign a Letter of Intent (LOI) to attend their chosen university. Many times these players go unsigned, or sign and never report, because they fail to meet the academic requirements. I believe this (in most cases) is an avoidable tragedy! Basketball has an early signing period in October, prior to the student-athlete's senior season, and a late signing period in April, well after their senior season ends. Signing periods for all the major team sports are listed in the appendix.

Whether we want to admit it or not, most parents recognize their children's shortcomings. If we are honest with ourselves, we can point out areas where our kids are not as strong. It is imperative that you, as Parent-Coach-Manager (PCM), recognize these shortcomings as quickly as possible and address them. PLEASE don't sweep them under the rug or expect your child to simply "grow out of it."

From an academic standpoint each of our children are very different. For the most part, school came pretty easy for Brennan. Camren has always had to work extremely hard for his grades. Jaylen is a mixture of the two – when she's organized and focused things come relatively easy. The challenge is keeping her organized and focused.

Very early in Brennan's academic career we noticed that he had to work harder in Math than English or Social Studies. We knew that writing and social sciences came easy for him. But he would need more time to complete assignments for his Math classes. Furthermore, when he took standardized tests in elementary and junior high, his reading/ writing scores were much higher than his math scores. Although he was able to maintain a "B" average in his math classes, it was what I refer to as a "hard B", meaning that he had to work really hard to get that "B".

On the other hand Camren struggled academically starting in second grade. He was placed in an Individual Education Program (IEP), which is a fancy way to say he received a LOT of extra help. In addition to the extra help he received in school, he attended the local Sylvan Learning

Center to get even more help. He was in an IEP from the second grade right through the sixth grade – which is when we finally started to see the light at the end of the tunnel. During these critical years Camren had a tough time in every subject except math. It was also during this time period that he developed study skills and habits that have made him an honor student. In fact, the title of the paper he wrote for acceptance into the National Honor Society (NHS) was "From IEP to NHS, the Camren Williams Story".

Once again, Jaylen is academically a combination of the two boys. Just like on the court, Jaylen has the ability to "flip the switch" and take her performance to another level. What we missed with Jaylen, is the fact that she is a lot more social than the boys. Furthermore, she's more easily distracted by (what I refer to as) non-essential things. You know, those things that seem important at the time but really don't amount to a "hill of beans" as my mother would say. So our "fight" with Jaylen is always about being organized, focused and prepared. We know that if she does this– good results will follow.

When you recognize these weaknesses early, you give yourself and your kid more time to correct the issue. Our plan for Brennan was to have him take the SAT early in his junior year. Our goal was to have him qualify academically during his junior year, and not to have these tests hanging over his head during his senior year. Two days after his junior season ended he took the test "cold" – meaning with no prep classes or tutors – to give us an indication. He actually scored high enough on the first attempt to qualify. But we already had a plan in place to take the test "cold" (without preparation) in December, then work with a tutor on a weekly basis for four months and retake the test in May of his Junior year. He improved his score by 120 points.

Some friends asked why we made him take the test again, since he had already qualified with the results from the first test. My reasons were simple, I explained to Brennan that the academic quality of the schools that had shown interest in him as an athlete was very high. At the time he was taking the test, some of the schools he had received offers from were, Stanford, Duke, Boston College, Wake Forest, Syracuse, and Michigan, all of which are highly-regarded institutions. I told him that when you walk onto the *campus of your choice* there are going to be students who will look at you and say, "he's only here because he's a football player." I want you to be able to look back at them and say that, "I qualified as an athlete, but I am also qualified as a student." I strongly believe that the word student should come first in the phrase "student-athlete". These young people must remember that they are students first and athletes second. Although they may be required (by the athletic program) to spend more time developing their athletic skills, they must always pay appropriate attention to their academics too.

There are countless books on SAT/ACT preparation. I have heard rumors (probably urban legends) that one test is easier for some than others, so I would suggest taking both. In fact, the same tutor that prepared the boys for their exams recommended that Jaylen take the ACT (instead of the SAT) because her skill set would allow for a better score. That said, there are a few things that you should be aware of when taking the tests. You can take the test as many times as you can financially afford (current cost $45). Looking at the Eligibility Center sliding scale, let's say your child's **Core** GPA is a 2.5, meaning they need an 820 total SAT score (Math and Critical Reading only). On the first try he or she scores a 400 and 350 on the math and reading sections respectively, totaling 750. When they retake the exam he or she scores 300 and 450 on the math and reading sections respectively, still totaling 750. At first glance you might think they're going to have to take the test again. Actually the results in their second exam have allowed them to pass the Eligibility Center with a score of 850. The NCAA will take the best scores from multiple exams, meaning they will take the 400 in math from the first exam and the 450 on the critical reading section from the second exam to total 850, thus making your son or daughter eligible.

This also applies to their core GPA. At my boy's school, Catholic Memorial (CM), if a student fails a class he receives a 55 for the term. If he re-takes the class in the summer and receives a 75, CM gives him an average of the two grades which is a 65, $(55 + 75 = 130$ divided by $2 = 65)$. The 65 equates to a D on the NCAA scale. However, the Eligibility Center will accept the 75 and ignore the failing grade or the averaged grade, thus giving the student a C. Every point counts and you should make sure you thoroughly understand how the Eligibility Center works.

We found great benefit in having Brennan work with a professional SAT tutor. She taught him all the secrets and tricks associated with maximizing his performance.   Ask for recommendations from your child's school, friends, or other students to find a tutor in your area. We have to get past the negative stigma surrounding tutors, coaches, or extra help. If Tiger Woods sees the necessity of having a coach, maybe it's a good idea.

Exposure (Highlight/Resumes/Recommendations) – Get on the Map!

The use of video can be a very useful recruitment tool, depending on your kid's sport. However, many PCM's don't know how to use video properly. Understanding your child's sport can go a long way toward creating an effective video presentation.

I am currently preparing for a speaking tour to areas of the country that are *not* recognized as football recruiting hotbeds. I open each seminar with the question, "If a tree falls in the forest and no one is there to hear it does it make a sound?" I believe the answer to that age-old question is, "yes it does make a sound, but unfortunately no one heard it." The sports version of this question is, "if an incredible athlete makes noise in an area where no one recruits – does he or she get a scholarship?" Unfortunately, the answer is probably NO! It is imperative that you get your athlete exposed to the highest level of play that they are capable of playing. The introduction of your kid's abilities to prospective colleges can be most efficiently done by sending film. A short film showing his specific talents is referred to as a "highlight film".

Virginia Union University Defensive Line Coach Emmanuel McNeil told me that he had never seen a bad highlight film. His point was that even a guy who couldn't "play dead" in a cowboy movie, could muster up 10 to 15 *good* plays over the course of their high school career. That said, putting together a good highlight film is a means of opening a door. Wake Forest Coach and Recruiting Coordinator Ray McCartney was the school's lead recruiter for Brennan. During a visit I asked Coach "Mac" how many highlight DVD's or videos he receives a week? He explained that during the busy time they get around *50* videos a day. I asked how many did he get a chance to see, he quietly replied "about 10% to 20%." Of the

250 highlight DVD's received, he gets to look at 25 to 50. Now in the "internet era" of recruiting – a student-athlete can send their highlights to a thousand schools with the click of a mouse. On the positive side, this can be a very efficient and cost-effective means of getting your kid's video out. On the negative side, now schools are now receiving hundreds of videos an hour! Yes that's right. In a recent conversation with Mark Pantoni, Director of Personnel at Ohio State, he shared that there are days when he has received more than 100 highlight reels to review. There is not enough time in the day for his staff to review the volume of films they receive.

Throughout this process I have learned a great deal about a lot of different schools. Other than our experience with North Carolina, there wasn't a better coaching staff and recruiting group than the coaches we dealt with at Wake Forest. Wake is a great academic institution, and the football program is also very good. With all due respect to their program and the school, if Wake Forest gets 250 DVD's a week, how many do you think USC, Florida, or Texas get? Probably thousands! Many PCM's are motivated by the Tom Brady story alluded to earlier, but they must realize that they are not the only highly motivated parent. In fact I would bet that nearly half of the more than 1,000,000 high school football players believe they have a future in college football. The reality is they might be able to play college football at the D2 or D3 levels.

I also learned that for basketball, video didn't play as big of a role in recruiting. I pulled Jaylen's highlights together throughout the years and would send it to schools – and rarely if ever did I get a response. When speaking to the coaching staff at Delaware (one of her unofficial visits) – I asked if Jaylen's video helped get her noticed by the staff. The recruiting director responded with a puzzled look on his face – "video, what video?" Thinking that this was a "fluke" I posed the same question to Providence College during a visit. And the Head Coach looked me squarely in the eyes and said – "we offered Jaylen based on how she moved in the pre-game warm-up line". Seriously, I replied. His come-back, "ABSOLUTELY!"

Your kid's sport, and the different aspects of that sport (position, event participation, etc.) will determine the importance of video. NCSA Recruiting Network has a great (free) link that gives good insight on what coaches need to see in highlight videos. The sight gives camera angles, shooting techniques, and directions for wide angle or close up shots – by sport and by position.

As I mentioned, I sent Brennan's highlight tapes to 20 different schools. I spent several hours combing through game film to find plays that showed his ability to play at the next level. I selected highlights and worked with a videographer to make a professional looking DVD. We put his statistics, his measurables, and contact information in the credits, and lastly we set it to music. In addition to the DVD I enclosed a copy of the bio outlined earlier.

Here comes the SARCASM! Because Brennan was *soooo* good, and made so many great plays, his highlight film was about 17 minutes long. There were nine minutes of offensive highlights, and eight minutes of defensive highlights. The offensive highlights had a combination of Jazz and Hip Hop music, while the defensive highlights were played over the "old standard" Jock Rock stadium music. I told you at the beginning of this book that I would share both the things I did "correctly" and the things I did "wrong".

Common sense would say that even the biggest college football staffs, with the largest football budgets, don't have the time and resources to watch 250 videos that are almost 20 minutes long. That would equate to more than 60 hours of film study, in addition to the film work necessary for them to prepare for their weekly opponent.

Second mistake, did I really think that the theme music would subconsciously trigger a scholarship offer. Most coaches have told me that when they are able to watch a DVD, they usually don't have the sound on. And when they do, they usually laugh and mock the music choices. One coach told me, "if he heard the theme from Rocky one more time he was *gonna* SCREAM."

Coaches have seen all of the tricks – slow motion, fast motion, repeating the same play from five different angles. A recruiter once told me that he had received what he thought was Pop Warner film. As an advisor to prospective athletes, I have seen videos that have been adjusted so that the players look "super" fast. This is easy to recognize by looking at the players on the side lines who are walking around as if they were speed walking. If I can tell, believe me, a college coach can tell when highlights have been tinkered with. Moreover, you lose credibility when you resort to such trickery.

I know parents who have sent highlights to the head coach, position coach, and the recruiting coordinator of *one* school – three DVD's to the same school. Most schools have a process whereby the highlights usually end up in the same place, no matter who they are addressed to. Fred Jackson, Michigan Assistant Head Coach, explained to me that they have the recruiting coordinator's assistant log all highlight films and distribute them to the potential position coach. If they like what they see, they will forward the highlight DVD to the area recruiter for his review. From there the DVD could come up in the weekly recruiting meeting and a plan would be made to contact the prospect. Or it could end up in some box, in some corner, never viewed by anyone. So how can you assure that your video is seen? You can't!

Just remember that recruiting is a process, and prospective players are discovered in a lot of ways. It may be the camp or combine or showcase your kid attended; it may be the highlight video; it may be their listing on a scouting service; or it could be that your athlete was discovered when a college recruiter was in your area scouting another prospect. More than likely, it will be a combination of all of these factors. You should do your best to cover as many of the bases as possible.

For football, I recommend that you use a highlight DVD or highly recognized video service like HUDL or XOS. And just like you would use a resume when applying for a job. I also advise you to use multi-system compatible DVD's or system links that allow the user to play it on a computer or tablet (as many staffs use IPads).

- Include an easy to read bio that will hopefully pique the interest of the receiving coach.
  - Make mention if your student-athlete is rated or listed on one of the recruiting services.
- Keep the video short, five to seven minutes.
  - Include Statistics and Measurables in the credits.
- Include a return card allowing the coach to request a full game film. Or a "receipt return" from your email.
- Include game film when the school requests information from you – (i.e. questionnaires)

For football, the best times to send film are between your son's Sophomore and Junior seasons. If possible, you should gather your son's Sophomore highlights and send highlights to schools that you are interested in. In addition, I recommend that you send film between each season that your son is playing on the varsity level. **The most important film is film from your son's JUNIOR YEAR; make sure you get it out as quickly as possible.** However, as the pace of recruiting accelerates sophomore film (Varsity level) will soon become THE year coaches want to evaluate. In addition to sending film to schools, it is imperative that you send film to scouting services like Rivals.com and Scout.com. They are tremendous resources for college recruiting. To be honest, it's best that your head coach send the films to both schools and the recruiting services. Coaches are viewed as more credible sources.

Although recruiting is a year-around part of college football, there are better times of the year to send your son's film. It's probably not a great idea to send film to Michigan the week that they are playing Ohio State.

In a lengthy discussion with Marion Hobby, Clemson Defensive Line Coach, regarding highlight films – I asked what are some important considerations with this critical part of the process? He explained that good editing, timing (when the film was received), and advanced notification were keys to getting your son's film seen.

Proper editing can make the difference in whether or not you get a response. Many parents and coaches put together a series of unorganized clips that show a bunch of great plays, but that don't tell a story. Editing is important for all positions, but it is critical for non-skill positions. I can take a running back's film and pull out 15 to 20 great runs and show that this player is a viable candidate. Linemen are different in that the lineman may have made a great block and had the ball carrier go the wrong way. Most would think that a lineman's highlights must match a successful outcome on the play. It helps, but it is not a necessity.

The most important consideration in editing highlight film is that it tells a story. The story should be told to show how this prospective athlete will fit into the college's program. Moreover, it needs to be broken down in terms applicable to your sport that allow the viewer to quickly assess your kid's ability.

116

Although the first edition of Brennan's highlight film was too long, it was impeccably edited. I worked for hours with the videographer to explain the story that I wanted to get across to potential schools. I was very specific in the types of plays that I wanted to show and relayed my ideas to him. Combining my football knowledge with his technical skills, we put together a story that told the viewer that the offensive/defensive lineman he was watching had the attributes required to play in their system. Instead of random highlights from his game film strung together without focus or definition, our film included the following:

Offensive Highlights	Defensive Highlights
Drive Blocking	Run Stops
Cut Off Blocking	Pass Rush
Cut Blocks	Tackles outside the box
Pass Protection	Big Plays
Pull/ Trap Blocks	Sacks/Tackles for Loss

When putting together Brennan's video I wanted prospective coaches to know that he was proficient at executing the techniques that their school's used. I put 6 to 10 plays into each category to show that he wasn't a one-play wonder. In hindsight, I could have reduced the number to 3 or 4 plays each to shorten the length of the video and still get the story told. Beyond this, I could have eliminated the music and the extra graphics. Remember, if your son is a drop back passing QB, don't send his passing highlights to a team that runs the Wishbone Option. Make sure his skills, and the skills on display are applicable to the schools that you send his film to.

Group highlights by skills. If your son is a running back use categories like inside runs, outside runs, pass catching. If your son is quarterback show his skills throwing deep passes, short passes, and running the ball. Remember, you are trying to convey a message of how your son will benefit their program.

As you can see understanding your kid's sport is critical. For Jaylen's (unwanted, unneeded, unnecessary videos - lol) I wanted to display her athleticism, her versatility. I separated plays by offense and defense. Secondly, I wanted coaches to see that she could play both inside (close to the basket) and outside effectively. Furthermore, I wanted them to see that she could run and jump. So there were plays in her reel that she literally did nothing except outrun everyone down the floor. Lastly, I picked plays that displayed competitiveness and toughness. For example diving for balls and fighting for a ball during a tie-up.

With all of my directorial and production efforts – none of the schools that offered her scholarship ever saw the video.

Although it's not completely related to the topic of highlight films – I feel it is important that parents of quarterbacks understand the obstacles they will face when trying to get QB's to the next level (especially D1). Over the years I have counseled several aspiring quarterbacks. It is **tough** to get into a D1 school as a QB prospect. Here's the reason, MONEY! As the amount of money paid to college football coaches has increased, the amount of time and patience programs have has decreased. Because the quarterback is the focal point of the program, college coaches don't have the time and resources to take a raw talent and teach him how to be a quarterback. Coaches are under tremendous pressure to win quickly, and are unwilling to place their coaching future in the hands of a novice.

Alex Kershaw was a player I coached in Pop Warner. In Alex's second year with me, I converted him from tailback to QB. He was the town's best basketball player and he was as tough as nails. After his Sophomore year, I sent his film to Mike Farrell at Rivals.com to get a professional assessment of his abilities. When I used to tell people about Alex, I would explain that this kid is 6' 3", 190 pounds and he was the National Punt, Pass and Kick runner-up when he was 12 years old. He can run, jump and throw – he could do it all. To explain how confident I was in his viability as a college QB, I would say, "If Alex Kershaw fully committed himself to football, he would be the best QB to ever come out of this state – In fact, DOUG FLUTIE would be (just) another name." The Flutie comment is borderline blasphemy in the state of Massachusetts. Actually, I just threw that in for dramatic effect, (and) to tick people off. The point is that Alex was not your average prospect. However, his highlight film received an average review.

Mike explained to me that he saw the raw ability that I saw, and that he could get to the next level. He noticed (what I already knew) that Alex didn't know how to read coverages, nor did he understand how to be a QB. He relied on his arm strength, and his superior athletic ability. He would throw the ball when his primary receiver was open, and run it when his first target was covered – this is a no-no for a QB and a sure sign that Alex lacked development.

If your son is a QB prospect, I would strongly suggest sending him to camps that specialize in developing quarterbacks and putting him in a high school program that has a great passing attack and has been successful in developing quarterbacks. The program doesn't have to send each player to a D1 school, but it should have players playing at the next level.

As you pull together your son's highlights, be mindful that you are trying to show that he can fit into the university's system. Pick plays that show your son's skills, toughness, and desire. Then, as previously suggested, group those plays into categories that are important to the prospective college.

For basketball, I would say that the point guard is "that" critical position. It's the position where an athlete may thrive in one system and struggle in another. As you go through the recruiting process for your athlete's sport, a key thing for you to understand is how their talents fit various systems at the next level.

Keep those Cards and Letters Coming

As you continue through the process, your kid will love running to the mailbox. Everyday is payday! Once you start receiving and returning questionnaires you will begin to get mail and more mail, and more mail. Schools recognize that you are getting mail from a lot of programs, so they will do everything they can to make you open their mail. It is their way of advertising what their school has to offer athletically, academically, and socially.

As a parent, pay attention to the mail because you will start to recognize what's important to the school. By that I mean, if you sort the mail and put each school into separate files, you will start to see a theme in the message they are trying to convey to your student-athlete. Each school will preach academics because very few people will say that education is not important. They will talk about their program, and the excitement surrounding the program. They will talk about the social amenities of the school, the campus, the girls or boys, the parties, even future networking.

Remember, the smaller the number of recruits a school is planning for, the more personal the mail will seem. Penn State sent a cartoon picture using Jaylen's head driving a car – when she received her driver's license. They sent notes to everyone in our immediate family letting them know how important Jaylen was to their program.

On any given day Brennan would receive mail from 15 to 20 schools. The volume of the mail can become quite daunting. My wife and I would review each piece of mail over the weekends or in some quiet time during the day. We took control of this task because Brennan had to focus on his school work and football (during the season). By taking this responsibility we saw firsthand the themes or "pitch" that schools were using to get his attention.

One (very good academic) school introduced itself to our family by sending a letter with pictures of girls on their campus with the headline "Prettiest Girls in _____ (their conference)". One school sent us a report stating that they were rated one of the country's "TOP PARTY SCHOOLS". Brennan never saw those letters as they went right into the trash. Now I am not naïve and I realize that girls and parties are a part of the college experience but that should not be the college's "lead in".

In addition to "snail-mail", schools now contact student athlete through email and social media. I will address social media in great detail later in the book.

Cards, letters, emails and social media contacts can also say a lot about a school. They not only show what's important at the institution, they also show how much homework they have done on you and your kid. If they continue to send you generic, non-personal information about their school, you will soon realize that they're not very serious about recruiting your student-athlete, or that they're not very good promoters.

Look for handwritten notes. Look for items specific to your kid's academic interest. Of all of the schools who sent my kids mail throughout the process, there were a few standouts. I have broken this outreach into phases, because as you get closer to a decision you will find more personal communication. A few words on each phase of the process follows:

Early Recruiting Phase

Rutgers University really knows how to grab your attention. They send mail in clear envelopes, using various sizes and the theme "R U AWARE" is on just about everything they send. R U as in "are you" also stands for Rutgers University. They did a very good job of stimulating our interest in a school we knew very little about. It was because of this approach that we were compelled to make two unofficial visits to learn more about their program. Colors also standout Florida's and Syracuse's Orange jump out of the pile of mail.

Middle Recruiting Phase

For football, the Virginia, Duke, Wake Forest and Boston College programs really stood out, as they were very good at making the "cold" process of recruiting very personal. Handwritten letters were always thoughtful and gave insight on the value placed on Brennan's recruitment. One day we received 33 postcards from Duke, 11 addressed to Brennan, 11 addressed to my wife, and 11 addressed to me. Using dark blue "Blue Devil" postcards we received one note from each coach, the athletic director, and recruiting director attempting to show how important Brennan was to their 2009 recruiting class. This personal touch was very flattering and would make the tough decision of not choosing to attend Duke even harder.

Ohio State, Penn State and North Carolina did a great job of moving from the cold informational communication to personal relationship developing mail. As previously stated, because the numbers are fewer basketball gets personal quicker.

Final Recruiting Phase

North Carolina, Boston College and Wake Forest were the standouts because in addition to the standard overview of the school they sent specific mail relating to his potential major. They made sure Brennan knew the potential for networking with their alumni. Furthermore, they outlined a plan and illustrated the opportunity for playing time at his position and showing him how he would fit into their respective programs.

Mail in the final phase for basketball is ALL personal, even acknowledges big events in the prospect's life (i.e. driver's license, 16th birthday, etc.).

The important thing about the mail is that *you as a parent* **must** stay involved. You really have to manage mail in a way that allows you not to become overwhelmed by the information. Recognize mail as the tool a school is using to introduce itself to you and your family. I wish I could say that I read every piece of mail sent, but I can't.

Lastly, one more warning about mail– don't be fooled by figures. As the old saying goes, "figures lie and liars figure." In the mail you will be bombarded by figures. I can't believe how many schools have the NUMBER 1 academic program, graduation rates, or number of players in the NFL. Amazingly enough, there were *at least* eight or nine programs that made claims to being best in each category. The reality is that you have to look the information up for yourself using a non-biased source like the NCAA website or other independent authorities like U.S. News and World Report's Top Colleges Edition.

Here is an example of how misleading figures were used in the recruitment of a young man I advise.

School: I thought you said academics are important to you?
Parent: They are, I want my son to get a great education.
School: Well why would you allow your son to go to school B with their poor academic performance?
Parent: What do you mean?
School: Take a look at these figures!

Graduation Rate Differential Report (African-American Student-Athletes)

School A	+8%	Number 1 in the country
School B	-5%	Number 80 in the country
School C	-1%	Number 63 in the country

Parent: Wow! I never knew that they were that bad.
School: What do you think?
Parent: I think we should consider your school

…As the great Paul Harvey would say "Here's the rest of the story"

School A told the truth in that their graduation rates for African-American Student-Athletes was 8% higher than those of White

Student-Athletes. While School B's graduation rates are 5% less and School C is only 1% lower.

STUDENT-ATHLETE GRADUATION RATE REPORT		
	WHITE	AFRICAN-AMERICAN
School A	43%	51%
School B	88%	83%
School C	98%	97%

Now which school would you want your child to attend? School A's +8% is still associated with a horrible overall 51% graduation rate. Are you kidding me? Only half the kids in their program graduate. Meanwhile the -5% is associated with a more respectable 88% graduation rate and the -1% is attributed to the highest graduation rate in the country.

Make sure you pay attention to the mail! If this school was good enough to trick a parent, how do you think your 18 year old will fare with this information?

Phone Calls

There are two types of phone calls during the recruiting process, both of which are very important in my opinion. The first kind of call your kid will receive is from the college coach recruiting him. Depending on the sport, the second type of calls are from the media. As the process intensifies, your phone may literally "ring off of the hook." Surprisingly, most of the calls will come from reporters. The number and frequency of calls from coaches are legislated by the NCAA. Calls from the media on the other hand can be virtually unlimited.

I say that both types of calls are important because they provide an opportunity for your son or daughter to communicate to the schools that have shown interest. Due to the fact that during most recruiting periods college football coaches are limited to one call per week, they use the media to keep their schools in front of prospective recruits. It is important for you (as a parent) to familiarize yourself with the members of the media and understand which schools they are linked to.

In football, during the month of May (actually mid-April to the end of May) of your son's junior year, coaches are allowed to make **one** call to introduce themselves and express their interest. This will be an exciting time in your household because the callers are usually head coaches who are household names. Our first call was from Al Groh – Virginia, followed by calls from Charlie Weis – Notre Dame, Rich Rodriguez – Michigan, Tom O'Brien – NC State, Jeff Jagodzinski – Boston College and Greg Schiano – Rutgers. The calls kept coming and coming and coming. This is an important call because it is the ONLY call the coach is allowed to make for the entire **Introduction Period.** So, they want to make a great impression. Some call the first day of the month to show you how important your son is as a prospect, while others call at the end of the month to try to make a "great" last impression. Either way, these calls are "big deals" and should not be taken lightly by your son. It's tough to be prepared, because you don't know when or who might call. However, you can do some preparation by taking notes from all of the questionnaires and contacts you've made. Most importantly, make sure your son is polite, respectful and expresses gratitude for the call and the caller's interest.

The quietest room in our house is the living room. It is out of the way of the daily family traffic flow and was the perfect place for Brennan to talk to coaches. Distractions are minimal, no TV, Playstation, computers, or other typical teen traps that may take your son's attention away from the potential $250,000 interviewer (coach) on the other end of the phone. Remember this may be your son's first communication with his next head coach and "you only get one chance to make a first impression."

One suggestion: (During Brennan's recruitment) Use your home phone number. Many recommend using their cell phone or any other number that you can turn off or ignore when the calls become too much. I chose to use our home number for three reasons: first I wanted to project the right image to the schools that were recruiting him, secondly my wife and I wanted to know, track and monitor who was calling, and lastly it allowed us to make sure that he was always in the right frame of mind and not distracted.

Using our home phone may have interrupted the flow of communication for the rest of the household, but we felt the positives outweighed the negatives. Using the home phone allowed us to stress that Brennan was a part of a family and that this was a family decision.

However, in today's recruiting world where there are so many points of access for your student-athlete. I would say it's more important to keep the lines of communication open between you and your child. Coaches, media, recruiting services reach out to kids through social media with great ease. In many cases it's their preferred mode of communication – largely because it's the kid's preference as well.

So having your student-athlete jot a note down whenever a coach or (anyone) involved in the process reaches out to them is a more than reasonable approach.

Coaches deal with kids from all kinds of backgrounds – two parent homes, single parent homes, kids who live with their grandparents, or guardians, etc. In addition to these situations, another growing phenomena are player "advisors". These "advisors" are also referred to as "street-agents", these potential predators used to be limited to basketball recruiting, but street-agents are now gravitating towards football recruiting. They serve as *self-proclaimed* advisors for the player, or the family, and often times position themselves as the go-between to the recruiter and the player and his family. Sometimes these advisors are tremendously valuable, honorable people working for the best interest of the prospect. HOWEVER, in most cases, they are unscrupulous characters looking for personal gain, usually in the form of MONEY!

It was extremely important for my kid's potential suitors to know they had a support system that would not tolerate the dirty side of the recruiting process. There were coaches who **only** liked to call them directly on their cell phones. With Brennan (unfortunately for them), was not your typical teenage boy who was "attached at the hip" to his cell phone. This meant that coaches were forced to contact him using our home number.

Two coaching staffs (who I will not name), called the house phone a couple times and asked to speak directly to Brennan, ignoring my wife on one occasion and me on another. After he spoke with the coaches, I asked "who they were" and "what did they say"? He named the schools and said that wanted his cell number to contact him directly, using the excuse that they did not want to disturb our family by calling the home number. Brennan obliged and gave them his number; but because he never answers his cell phone – they were met with the frustrating need to call the house phone to reach him. One staff, after leaving 20 or 30 messages on his cell phone, gave up – without ever trying to call him on our home number.

My wife and I found it interesting that these coaches viewed calling our home number as "bothersome" to our family, instead of looking at it as an opportunity to get to know our family. This "barrier to entry" allowed us to eliminate programs that weren't comfortable with dealing with a strong family. I saw such calls as a blatant attempt to isolate Brennan and get him to make a decision independent of his family – which was NOT going to happen!

It's interesting to note that during Jaylen's contact period coaches called Jaylen on her cell phone, and a few days later they'd call me or my wife – "just to catch up". I think there needs to be this kind of balance, as much as my 17 year daughter would like to think she's independent and needs no parental oversight in this process. I believe it's absolutely critical that parents/guardians stay involved.

In this part of the process, (one call per month phase) we felt it was important to monitor who called, when they called, and how many times they called. If a coach broke this simple "one call rule," there was no telling what other rules he might break. During these calls, you can get a real sense of the integrity of the program. One example was a call from (former) Wake Forest Head Coach Jim Grobe, who called when Brennan was not home. I talked with Coach Grobe for about 15 minutes and learned something about a program that I knew very little about. At the end of the conversation, *he asked* if Brennan could give him a call soon, because NCAA rules did not allow him to call back. This was a "little thing", but a "big thing". Technically, he never spoke with Brennan, but he had talked to me. So by NCAA rules, the ONE CALL for the month was made and Coach Grobe's program had the integrity not to violate either the *spirit* of the rule, or the letter of the rule. The integrity of Coach Grobe and his staff was one of the key reasons that Wake Forest was one of the final three schools we considered.

A lot of people were surprised that Wake Forest was one of the "hats" on the table when Brennan was making his announcement. However, we were determined to stick to the core values we had established when the recruiting process began. Many thought we should have put Florida, Notre Dame, or Michigan on the table because they were great schools with bigger football programs. But it was truly a pleasure getting to know Coach Grobe and his staff throughout the process. It can be very challenging to stay grounded and not get caught up in the hype of the "big time" football programs when they come calling. Before the process takes on a life of its own, jot down the things that are important to you and your family. Then look at the note each week to remain focused.

The second type of phone call that your son (and family) will have to deal with are calls from the media. Especially in football and men's basketball! This is how it works – as previously stated, a school is only allowed to call you one time during the 45 or so key recruitment days in April and May, and just once a week from September to December. But, schools will also give your son's contact information to their local media outlets to allow them to conduct interviews. The bigger the school, the more the media! These media outlets are sometimes local newspapers, but more often, they are associated with online scouting services. Rivals.com, 247 Sports, ESPN Recruiting and Scout.com are the major players in the game. These scouting services assign writers to each school. Those writers will call to find out the level of interest you may have in their program, also allowing them to update their readership on your son's recruitment.

These calls seem like a manageable scenario until you do the math. There were about 30 schools that offered Brennan, and another 10 to 15 schools that expressed interest. Let's just use the round number of 40 schools with an average of 3 media sources per school.

Call Source	Calls
Coach Calls	40
Media Outlet 1	40*
Media Outlet 2	40*
Media Outlet 3	40*
Total Calls	**160**

* Remember there is NO LIMIT to the number of calls made by Media Outlets

With up to 200 calls per month or seven to 10 calls a day it can be quite overwhelming for a high school **student** who has homework, football practice, workouts, and a social life. The NCAA does not oversee contact made by media outlets.

Therefore the number of calls you may receive from these sources is unlimited.

At the beginning of the section, I said that both types of calls were important and they are! Although the previous outline shows how calls from the media can become a nuisance – you need to realize that they can be very useful. At the outset of the calling phase of his recruiting, I noticed that Brennan was very uncomfortable with the interviews. Most of his discomfort was because he didn't feel informed or prepared. For Brennan, answering these calls was like showing up for a test that he hadn't studied for.

Quick story:

Between Brennan's Sophomore and Junior season, we scheduled an Unofficial Visit to Penn State. This visit would take place two days before his participation at the Nike Camp being held at Penn State. I contacted the area recruiter, Bill Kenney, and asked him to set up a school tour. Coach Kenney put together a great itinerary and faxed it over to me a couple days prior to our departure. Brennan saw the fax and inquired about some of the names on the schedule. The first name was Wally Richardson, a former PSU quarterback who served as a member of the academic staff. Kermit Buggs, the recruiting coordinator was the second name that Brennan didn't recognize. Bill Kenney, the offensive line coach (whom Brennan had briefly met) was the next name he questioned. As he perused the remaining schedule, he paused and asked, "Dad, this last meeting… how do you say this name, P-P-PA-PA-TEER- NO, who is he?"

After explaining that "he" was the "winningest" coach in college football history, that he was the same man who coached Uncle Michael (Timpson) – his Godfather, and the guy who was the coach in the movie we saw, *"Something for Joey"*, he responded, "WOW he coached that long, no wonder he's won so many games." He had no clue!

The reason Brennan didn't feel comfortable on the interviews was because he did not want to get caught not knowing the head coach's name, or some of the important history surrounding their program. And if he didn't know the great Joe Paterno, how could he know Greg Schiano, Jim Grobe, or Jim Tressel?

128

So to prepare him, I put together a spreadsheet listing all of the pertinent information he would need during the call. I also taught him to take his time and answer questions completely and clearly. These are job interviews. You want your son to come across as intelligent, articulate, and interested in whomever is on the other end of the phone. By empowering Brennan with information, he became more relaxed and was able to clearly and concisely state his interest in a program.

The media is a powerful force. It can be used both to build and to destroy. Use it as a tool to build your son's image by preparing him for interviews. Because these interviews are rarely scheduled in advance, you have to be ready at a moment's notice – so get those "cheat sheets" ready. I am convinced that Brennan received four or five additional offers because of his impressive interviews that were posted on recruiting websites. For example, a school may not think that your son has an interest in going (far) away to school, but if they read on their big rival's (no pun intended) website that a kid is considering them – they may do some additional homework to see if this kid could possibly help their *own* program.

There *will* be a point where the phone calls may overwhelm you and your son. It is important to keep the lines of communication open (between you and your son) so that you recognize when (or if) he needs a break from the deluge of calls. During his Senior year, to manage calls and maintain sanity, we informed coaches that Brennan accepted calls on Sundays and Mondays **only**. This served a few purposes, as it allowed our son to focus on his school work and "have a life". In addition, I didn't want him doing interviews or thinking about college football the night before he had his high school football games. By limiting the calls, we allowed Brennan to relax Tuesday through Saturday and just be a 17 year old high school Senior. Some have considered the boundaries I imposed as too strict and felt it may have cost him additional opportunities. I believed that it was more important that we balanced the responsibilities of Brennan being a high profile recruit and enjoying his last year of high school.

I have to say most schools honored our request. Those that didn't somehow got the hint when we didn't answer the phone. THANK GOD FOR CALLER-ID! Just remember to take control of this part of the process. Most importantly, make sure that you and your son realize that there are probably a million other high school football players who would love to have coaches calling them. Besides, if your biggest problem in life is someone calling you and offering your son 250 grand, I'd say life is pretty good!

It may also serve to remember that this was just a few short years ago. With the current pace of technology, schools will soon avail themselves of even more "radical" portals to reach out to kids. I'll bet that that by the time I write my future edition "Recruit My Grandkid" – coaches will be using virtual images like "holograms" to communicate with prospects. Imagine walking into your kid's room and seeing a hologram of Nick Saban, Rick Pitino or Geno Auriemma "standing" ready to greet you. The technology is already in place; and trust me, the coaches are just waiting on the NCAA to grant them permission to use it.

Social Media

I would be negligent if I didn't address the topic of Social Media as it relates to your kid's recruiting. I could write an entire book on this topic alone. I put this critical point at the end of this quarter, and just before our 4th and final quarter – The Selection Process because if you miss this the game could end here.

Most parents realize that their children use social media to communicate with their friends and family. During my speaking engagements countless parents have stated concerns about their kid's connection and or obsession with social media. They (like me) are bothered by the amount of time their kids waste interacting on these portals. They (validly) worry about exposure to strangers, and the other dangers that this communication medium avails. All of those are legitimate concerns. But I am going to focus on the role social media can play in your kid's potential recruitment.

Let me start by saying that I am not a parent who is against social media. I don't judge those parents who forbid their children access to these mediums. I just view it as a sign of the times, it's the way people communicate. I am sure that "way back when" – some parents had issues to communicating by phone. They may have believed that communication should only be done "in-person". Well I just look at social media as the way this generation communicates.

Social Media is more than a bunch of message boards where people post pictures, quote sayings, or express thoughts. Social Media is so important to the recruiting process that many colleges have established special departments that have ONE JOB! That job is to monitor the social media pages of their current and future athletes. They literally have someone sitting at a desk in an office reading the thoughts and expression of every 16 to 23 year old that is (or could potentially be) a part of their athletic program. "SHOOT ME NOW", was my first response to hearing of this arduous responsibility.

As previously stated, Camren and Armani attend Ohio State, which is coached by Urban Meyer. I was shocked to learn that they have a staff that monitors social media. Moreover, they will NOT offer a prospect a scholarship until someone on that staff has reviewed the athlete's social media pages.

Social Media is now a part of the Athletic Questionnaire. Most think of it as just a way that the school can communicate with you. True, but it's much more far-reaching. They believe it's another way for them to see what type of kid you have. A recruiting director once told me that "if a kid is stupid enough to post something bad on his *facebook* page, we don't want him for two reasons". First, "when we see something in poor taste on his page, we can only assume that he's doing things that are a lot worse." Secondly, "if he's stupid enough to post it, then he ain't smart enough to be here!"

What can a bad post cost you? Well it cost one very high profile recruit a scholarship to both Michigan and Notre Dame. This young man was a top 50 recruit – with scholarship offers to nearly every major football program. And he had these offers rescinded because of posts he made to his *Twitter* and *facebook* accounts.

Student-athletes need to realize that if a school invests $250K in to you, they have the right to expect you to represent the school positively.

Social Media or social networks can be used as a powerful tool when used wisely and responsibly. It's an excellent opportunity for your son or daughter to market themselves to college coaches.

If social media is a window into the life of your student-athlete they can divulge images that can paint a positive picture of themselves. Posting pictures or writings that show their love for their (chosen) sport. Displaying things about family, school, values and social consciousness can go a long way toward giving colleges confidence that your kid is a trustworthy investment.

Remember in virtually all NCAA team sports, there are only a limited number of scholarship spots available. Your son or daughter is competing with all of the athletes that play *their* position in *their* sport… **Everything** counts!

Fun Fact: One of Camren's first assignments after being hired as a Scout by the Patriots was to research EVERY potential 2016 draft pick's social media accounts. Furthermore, it was not (just) their recent history, he had to go back FIVE YEARS in their accounts. Do the math, the Patriots weren't just concerned about the social media posts from the prospect's college years, five years – looks at their high school years.

Question: What does your son or daughter's social media accounts say about them?

Contact Periods

Because sports have different seasons, the NCAA establishes different contact periods by sport. These contact periods are often changed or adjusted. Understanding the contact periods for your student-athlete is very important for you to know. In addition to allowing different contact periods by sport, the NCAA also has different contact periods by college divisions within each sport. The most accurate information regarding contact dates are available on the NCAA website.

This doesn't seem like a lot, but remember… football coaches are allowed to visit your son's school up to 3 times per year. They can increase the number of visits by using the visits for academic evaluations and athletic evaluations. In addition they can visit the school to meet with your son's coaches, academic advisors and counselors.

These are *very interesting* visits because no matter what the coaches were there for, they always seemed to wander the halls and bump into Brennan. A quick handshake and exchange of pleasantries and they were off to meet with his coach. The (tongue in cheek) *"accidental"* contact with Brennan didn't count against the allowable contacts although it was a brief encounter with the prospect. One coaching staff was *really* good, they would schedule visits to his school at the end of the school day – to meet with his strength coach. In the WEIGHT ROOM! Hmmm, I wonder where Brennan would be every day after school? He'd better be in the WEIGHT ROOM! Needless to say that coaching staff had a 100% "bump into" rate.

Basketball contacts are a lot different. Coaches flock to Spring and Summer AAU tournaments to scout, and monitor prospective athletes. Although these are not contact periods coaches use these periods to show "face". Remember basketball recruiting is a lot more personal, if you are a player and you see John Calapari (men's basketball) or Geno Auriemma (women's basketball) on the sideline it's just as good as a personal contact. Often times these sightings are better than a personal visit. In the competitive world of recruiting, athletes know who the "high profile" players are and they know if Calapari or Petino are there to see a kid like Nerlens Noel it is a statement confirming that the player is a legitimate prospect.

High profile coaches create a buzz in the gym, and everyone knows that they are there to see the big name player. However, a lot of players get discovered because of their performance as a teammate or opponent of the primary recruiting target.

Basketball coaches visit schools, attend AAU club practices, do in- home visits, reach out to kids through social media, texts, email, snail mail and of course phone calls. You name a way to see and talk to prospects and they will use it!

4th Quarter: The Selection Process

So, you have now reached the point in the journey where your "team" has to make a decision. Your kid has multiple scholarship offers. The smile you're wearing is derived from a combination of his growth and accomplishments, and the extra money you'll have, because you won't have to pay for that all-important education.

What's the right choice? What's the right academic fit? Which coaching staff do we like? What is the campus like? The number of possible questions impacting this decision is infinite. Remember, this is not a 4 year decision; it's a 40 year decision! I mean to say that this decision will set the course of your young person's life for the next 40 years, maybe even for the rest of their life. By the way, you will hear that "4/40" line about a thousand times – throughout this process.

Corwin Brown, Defensive Coordinator at Notre Dame, gave Brennan some great advice. He told my son not to fall for a recruiting pitch. By that Coach Brown meant, don't choose a school because a coach had a good "line" or showed you some great facilities. He reminded Brennan that ALL of the schools he was considering were great schools and that he could be successful at any of them. The coach also told Brennan that all he had to do was to find the school where he felt most comfortable. This eliminated a lot of anxiety for Brennan, because he no longer had to worry about picking **the** school that would afford him success, *as if* there is only **one** possible school. Once that pressure was out of the equation, all he had to do was find a school where he felt comfortable as a student, as a football player, and socially.

Another person who shared sound counsel was Matt Alkire, Northeast Regional Scout/Reporter for Scout.com, who told Brennan to pick a school he would love to attend if his career ended the first day of practice. Football (for the most part) will take care of itself. So, if your kid's choice is solely based on their sport, they'll be forgetting about the other very important aspects of the college experience.

These principles are universal in the world of recruiting. Once your son or daughter has an idea of the type of school they want to attend, i.e. academic fit, social fit, size, rural or urban setting etc., the selection then becomes mostly about relationships.

Nor is it just about the obvious coach to player relationships. Teammates, (non-athlete) classmates, advisors, and support staff are also key people that need to be considered.

When Jaylen committed to Penn State, the summer after her freshman year, there was (only) one player on the PSU roster that would (still) be on the team when she arrived in 2015. The coaching staff explained, that although the players would be different when she arrived — the roster would be comprised of the same "type" of kids and personalities.

Penn State Head Coach Coquese Washington is an amazing person. In addition to being a great coach, she has a law degree from Notre Dame. Her accomplishments on and off of the court are numerous — but most impressive to us is her commitment to her family. As the mother of two young children she explained one of her core recruiting values. Due to of the amount of time that her children spend around the team — Coach Washington won't recruit a player that she doesn't feel could "babysit" her kids. It gave us great comfort to know the type of teammates Jaylen would have when she arrived in State College, three years after committing.

At the end of the day, your son or daughter has to feel comfortable with the school. In my experiences, if the school works, the sport works. Simply put, the more comfortable they are in the overall school environment, the more productive they will be on the field, court, track or pool.

Stop those cards and letters, PLEASE!

Okay, okay, I admit it...there will come a time when you have seen enough cards, letters, and school paraphernalia – a point where the mail you once relished becomes a source of aggravation. My wife and I managed the mail for Brennan because we felt it was too much for a high school student athlete. However, our initial neat and orderly filing system turned into a 4 by 4 foot moving box of cards and letters that we planned to (but never did) review. As I tossed the unopened mail into this box, I often thought of the poor kid who would die to get just one of these letters affirming his football ability. Nevertheless, into the box we tossed.

Add to this constant stream of snail mail, the NCAA's allowable social media contacts from coaches and program assistants. It seems as if the information and communication cycle is virtually unending. Tweets, direct messages, *facebook* Inbox notes, Instagrams, creative Snapchats and a host of other media is relentlessly employed by skillful recruiters.

In my own 1982 recruiting experience, there was mail and occasional phone calls to my house. Our phone did not have call waiting. Years later, we were compelled to limit Brennan's contact by limiting access to his cell phone number. Just three years after Brennan's odyssey – Camren and Armani were bombarded by cell phone calls as it became even more challenging to limit access. Yet another three years passed and recruiters would now seek to access Jaylen through social media, cell phone, mail, email, calls to her high school coach and her AAU coaches.

My suggestion, embrace the communications phase. Control it as best you can; but don't avoid it. This is a part of having an elite athlete that is in high demand. Each one of those calls, letters, messages or "tweets" is from someone trying to **give** you $250,000. So, I'm sure you've had worse annoyances.

Narrowing Down

It is imperative that you and your kid set deadlines. Earlier I alluded to the June decision deadline that I set for Brennan. Although his eventual choice was not in that list of 6 "final" schools – I am convinced that he never would have found North Carolina if we hadn't eliminated the other schools. It is in the elimination or narrowing down process where you will begin to see the type of school your son likes.

It is imperative for you to be honest with those schools that show interest in your athlete. A lot of prospects hoard scholarships. They are more interested in finding out how many offers they can get than trying to find the right school. I explained to my kids that it was important that they notify schools (who had offered scholarships) when they were no longer interested in their program. Recruiting is a tough job, and the sooner you let a school know that you don't have an interest, the sooner they can move to the next person on their list. I felt it was important my kids understood that their indecisiveness may cause another deserving prospect a lot of anxiety. For example, one of the offers Brennan received late in the process was from Florida. (Then) Coach Urban Meyer (current Ohio State Head Coach) called Brennan's head coach to express interest in Brennan and to offer a scholarship. I explained to Coach Meyer that I would talk to Brennan about their offer and that we would get back to him as soon as possible. Because of the timing of the offer, I realized that Brennan was not the first defensive lineman Florida had offered – and with a little research, I found out that one of their targeted recruits had committed to Oklahoma. I logically made the assumption that my son was next on the list. We were not offended by Florida's late offer, after all they fit the qualifications of our "approved list" of schools, good academics, good football program – but we didn't feel that there was enough time left in the process to *really* get to know the program. So I called the (then) area recruiter, Steve Addazzio (now Head Coach at Boston College) and explained that we were not interested, which allowed Florida to move to the next person on their list.

As soon as we walked off of the Notre Dame campus, Brennan told me that he really didn't care for the school. I explained this to Coach (Corwin) Brown and he asked us to wait before eliminating them from consideration. We agreed to his request for two reasons; first, Notre Dame is a great school with tremendous educational value; and secondly, Notre Dame is what I refer to as an **Influential Recruiting School** – meaning, if Notre Dame Football offers your son, he will probably have his choice of any school in the country. Moreover, the same would apply to UConn, Notre Dame, Duke or Stanford Women's Basketball. A lot of schools will offer your son or daughter, just because they saw an offer from Notre Dame. A former teammate of mine told Brennan that he HAD to consider attending Notre Dame because there is "No such thing as an *unemployed* Notre Dame graduate." During his visit Head Coach Charlie Weis explained to Brennan that no school could compare to Notre Dame when it came to the 40 year decision he was going to make. Most schools require football players to room together during their first year in the program, while Notre Dame requires football players to room with a non-athlete. The reason is two-fold. It's a pretty big deal for a "regular" student to room with an ND football player. On the other hand, the roommate that the player gets is expected to be one of tomorrow's leaders, thus benefiting the football player on the "40 year decision" side of the equation.

Narrowing down schools is challenging because you are going to say **no** to some great programs. During the process you meet some great people. Brennan became very close to some of the coaches who were recruiting him. One coach used to tell Brennan that he was the kind of kid the coach wants his son to grow up to be. Another coach used to call and tell him that he would keep in touch with him even if he chose to go to another school – "friends for life". A coach's wife told him that she would be his "Mom" away from home.

Over time he developed relationships with a lot of people, most of whom he would have to disappoint. Because

Brennan could only select one school, there were 30 relationships he would have to reject. This was equally tough on our family also as we developed relationships with different coaches. My wife used to say that those coaches with "southern accents" seemed so nice.

It was hard for Brennan to say no to a school because he thought he would hurt their feelings. I explained to him that it (the recruiting process) was a business and that although programs would prefer to hear a YES – they'd rather hear a NO, than a "I DUNNO" or a "MAYBE".

Recruiters are in the business of creating relationships out of thin air. Really good recruiters do their homework. With the advent of Google, you can find a ton of information on a prospect and in many cases, his family too. As a former NFL player, there is a lot you can learn about me and my family with the click of a mouse.

The first phase of narrowing down the final decision list is getting the number of schools being considered down to a manageable amount. The number becomes manageable when you can handle the calls, handle the mail, handle the visits and get to know the programs at a deeper level.

We went from roughly 25 schools down to 6. Our goal was to get to five schools by June of his Junior year. Five was not a random number. It was consistent with the number of Official Visits. I felt that if Brennan could reduce the number to five – he could make his visits and pick the best fit from there. Trimming to five gave us clarity and it allowed Brennan to try to get to know his recruiter and his prospective position coach, which in some cases was a totally different person.

Narrowing the possibilities down from 25 or so programs to 6 was pretty easy, but reducing the number to 3 was extremely tough. By this point, the better coaches had a good rapport with Brennan; but they also knew my son Camren and daughter Jaylen. They knew Camren was a good football player and would call and joke with him – saying that the only reason they were recruiting Brennan was to get to him. My daughter Jaylen was 11 years old and about 5' 10". So they would talk to her about their women's basketball program and how great it would be if she went to their school. At the time we had no idea that she was really paying attention. The really good coaches are master relationship builders!

Brennan took his first Official Visit to Virginia and had a great time. He enjoyed hanging with his host and, interestingly, his host also invited Camren (then 14) to hang out with the college kids during the visit. We enjoyed the game as Virginia beat North Carolina in overtime. Since we visited schools that were playing against schools that were also recruiting Brennan – we made a rule. We would cheer for the school that "paid the bill" which was of course, the school hosting our visit.

Attending games where the opponent is also in consideration is interesting. You get to see how that program operates in a hostile environment. The most interesting thing is that the visiting team is NOT allowed to speak to you. The host team usually invites players onto the field during the pregame warm up and there are ample opportunities for you to speak to both the host and the opponent. Coaches cannot make personal contact with players while they are visiting another school. Talk about awkward! Brennan is standing on the field and two feet away is Sam Pittman (currently coaching at Georgia), the Offensive Line Coach and lead recruiter from North Carolina, and NO ONE SAID A WORD! That showed me a lot! It showed me that Coach Pittman had respect for the process. It also showed me that they were a program with integrity.

During his visit to another school (purposely left nameless) the visiting team's coach walked over to Brennan and almost scolded him for considering the hosting school. It was a totally disrespectful act that pretty much eliminated this school from contention.

After Brennan had completed his third visit he told me that he had had enough. Dad, he quietly whispered, "I am tired of visiting, let's make this the last one." I convinced him to take one more trip to the local school (Boston College) out of respect. He didn't feel a visit was necessary because he had spent a lot of time at the school; but I thought he needed to show that he was serious about considering BC. An Official Visit is a gesture of sincere interest.

Brennan took four of his potential five official visits. I wanted him to save one visit just in case plans with the school he decided to attend fell apart. After completing the visits, my wife and I gave him about a week to reflect on the time spent on each campus.

We sat down and had Brennan adjust the numbers on the spreadsheet. Without letting him see the totals I continued to quiz him. The final three were obvious; but there was not a big difference between them. So we discussed the merits of each school. It started to clear up. One school began to stand out. Finally he said, "I think I am leaning towards North Carolina."

According to our established plan, for the next 15 minutes my wife and I tried to talk him out of going to UNC. She focused on the emotional – the distance, the difference in culture... I focused on the football program – the position they planned for him to play. We reviewed the academic platform of the UNC School of Journalism and made *him* explain why it was the right fit educationally. Finally, I asked him the big question – "which school would you choose if you couldn't play football?" He looked me directly in the eyes and said, "I would go to Carolina."

I again would suggest that their exposure to Brennan's recruitment made the process for Camren and Armani a lot easier. Since we did most of the visits as a family – they became very comfortable with recruiting. Moreover, they knew very early on exactly what they were looking for. Unbeknown to us was the fact that on the periphery of all this football recruiting, eleven year old Jaylen was also paying attention. All three kids would use Brennan's experiences to help determine what type of school they would like to attend.

Biblical wisdom says "Let your yes, be yes!" So that was our family rule for recruiting. In our minds, a verbal commitment was as good as "signing" your name on the dotted line. I told Brennan, prior to his verbal commitment to UNC, that it would take a catastrophic event for me to allow him to change schools.

In this day and age where kids often commit and de-commit several times during the recruitment process – I wanted my kids to take their VERBAL COMMITMENT seriously.

Once again, Camren and Armani were ahead of the game. Schools knew who they were earlier and the boys knew what they wanted sooner. They committed to Penn State in the Spring and Summer of their Junior year respectively. They both were given the same warning that Brennan received, each one told "Unless something catastrophic happens, you're going to Penn State".

Little did we know that we would be forced to exercise the *decommitment* option because of the horrific events that hit the PSU football program during the Fall of their senior year. I'm of course referring to the Jerry Sandusky child abuse case, where a former coach and long-time program associate was convicted of child molestation. That case changed everything that Penn State Football was known for almost overnight.

Many in the recruitment environment felt that Camren and Armani were a package deal, a reasonable assumption since they have been attached at the hip since the third grade. However, our approach was different. Our goal for "project #2" and "#2.5" was to find the right school for both of them individually. If it happened to be the same school that would be great. Still, the focus was finding the right school. Now I would be disingenuous if I told you we didn't hope they'd attend the same school. Furthermore, I'll be totally honest in saying that had the landscape not changed so dramatically at North Carolina, I think both Camren and Armani would have become Tar Heels.

I believe that they would have selected UNC largely because of the relationships that they developed during Brennan's time there.

Regarding Penn State, as the unfortunate events began to unfold, I instructed both Cam and Armani to refrain from changing their commitment until we had more information. Frankly, I was also concerned that if Camren were to decommit it would cause several other players to leave PSU. I don't say that out of any sense of arrogance. The simple truth is that Camren had become a lead recruiter for PSU in his own right.

Camren was the second player to commit in the 2012 graduating HS class. Following his own commitment to Penn State, he took it upon himself to reach out to as many good players as he could, in order to convince them that PSU was the place to go. It really became a job for him. He would talk to the PSU coaching staff and ask about prospects. Then he'd find them on Facebook or Twitter and make his pitch. He was determined to make the 2012 PSU class great. After all, there are no NCAA limits to the amount of contacts another athlete could (or can) make on behalf of a school.

Responsible is too strong of a word, so let's say Camren was highly influential on 14 of the (then) 20 PSU commits. In fact, when the "Sandusky" dust cleared and we allowed Camren and Armani to change their commitment, 5 of those recruits joined them at Ohio State. At the time I was not sure what Camren's post-football playing life would be; but I was right by guessing that he wouldn't stray too far from the game.

After the PSU fallout and Camren's return to the recruitment process, I asked him were there any other schools he would consider. As you can imagine, when the news began to spread about PSU – coaches were aggressively trying to reach out to both boys. Admittedly, more schools called for Armani than Camren, but many inquired about both. I asked both boys which schools they'd like me to return calls to? Camren quickly answered, "there is only one, Ohio State!" Armani, was a little less certain and listed a few, none of which was Ohio State.

When the scandal at PSU initially hit, former Ohio State Coach Mike Vrabel called our high school coach and made a very respectful inquiry. He said simply, "I have just been hired at my alma mater, Ohio State, and I am late to the recruiting process. I would like to let Camren Williams know that if he re-opens his recruitment, Ohio State would be interested in having him visit." OSU needed linebackers from the 2012 class. They had just 1 commitment and wanted at least 3.

At the time, Ohio State didn't express interest in Armani. They were actually full at his position. In point of fact, it was unclear on which side of the ball Armani would play. Notre Dame and Boston College wanted him as a slot receiver, while Michigan liked him as a cornerback. All told, about 10 schools reached out to Armani. Meanwhile, there were about 5 that inquired for Cam. Due to the lateness in the process, I asked Armani to narrow his focus to the schools that he had SERIOUS interest in seeing. He said, Michigan, Notre Dame and (if they were interested) he'd always liked Ohio State.

At the time it looked like their hope of going to the same school wouldn't materialize. After repeatedly sending information to Ohio State, the school remained unsure about whether they'd have the ability to offer Armani. With that door seemingly closed, we focused our attention on Michigan and Notre Dame.

As you can see, both Camren and Armani wanted to play in "high profile" football schools. Nothing against, schools like Wake Forest, Maryland, or Boston College – but these boys wanted to experience a school that was known for its FOOTBALL! They both loved big schools, and loved the idea that they could potentially play in front of 100,000 people.

Armani soon began to feel closer and more comfortable with Michigan's plan for him. So it began to look like the two boys who'd always been so close might soon line up on opposite sides of (arguably) the greatest rivalry in collegiate athletics. During a visit with Armani, Greg Mattison, Michigan's Defensive Coordinator suggested this exact scenario, saying,

"How great will it be for the two brothers to play against each other in the greatest college football rivalry?"

As our family started to become more comfortable with the boys being at different schools, and *rival* schools at that, we received a call from Ohio State, asking if Armani had made a decision. They then informed us that Everett Withers, the coach who'd tried to them to North Carolina was going to be joining the Ohio State staff. We had known Everett for 4 years, and were very comfortable with him. So just as Armani was about to make his decision final, Everett asked him to come for a visit and "kick the tires" at OSU. Armani took his official visit, with his mother and aunt. Of course Camren jumped at another chance to visit the school, so my wife also attended. Since Camren and I had already taken his official visit to Ohio State, we had to pay for my wife and Camren's second trip.

Recalling Brennan's first day at UNC, as we tearfully left the school and left Brennan behind – 11 year old Jaylen announced that she had made a decision on the school that she was going to attend. She said she with missing her brother, tears streaming down her face, "I am going to North Carolina!" We carefully explained that Brennan would be long gone by the time she could attend UNC and that she did not have a scholarship offer to UNC. Again, family considerations make all of this as difficult a time, as it is an exciting one.

During Brennan's three days of orientation to UNC, we took full advantage of our time in Chapel Hill. Camren and Armani attended the UNC football camp, while Jaylen visited with the Women's Basketball staff and team.

As the boys were competing for attention on the football field, Jaylen had the opportunity to get to know some of the coaches and players. Although her commitment declaration wasn't quite realistic, it wasn't outside of the realm of possibility. The coaches were great. They gathered information on her summer schedule and promised to see her play during the July viewing period.

After getting over the emotion of leaving her big brother behind, Jaylen stated that she liked UNC almost as much as she liked Penn State. "Penn State?"…my wife quizzed. "Why Penn State?" Jaylen replied that of all the schools she'd ever seen that Penn State was her favorite.

Now picture the same scene a few years later as we are tearfully leaving Camren and Armani behind at Ohio State. With tears again streaming down her face, Jaylen announces that she's going to Ohio State.

Yet this time things were different! An hour before leaving the Ohio State campus, Jaylen had received an offer from (then) Women's Basketball coach Jim Foster. As a 9th grader, Jaylen was now 6' 3", and was rated as one of the top 50 players in the 2015 graduating class. Furthermore, if she did attend Ohio State, the boys would still be there.

Once again, we took advantage of our time during the boys' orientation to allow Jaylen to get a feel for the OSU Women's Basketball program. During our drive home, as emotions began to subside, we began to realize that she had just received her first scholarship offer.

To be honest, we had a feeling that she would get an offer during that month; but we didn't expect it to be from Ohio State. After dropping the boys off, our plan was to make an unofficial visit to the University of Delaware. Based on conversations with her high school and AAU coach, we suspected that they might offer during her time on campus. She also had a visit scheduled to Boston College when we returned home to Massachusetts.

By this time, all the mail we were receiving and the calls her coaches were getting, led us to believe that her performance during the Spring Showcases was garnering sincere accolades.

As we arrived on the Delaware campus for our morning meeting with Head Basketball Coach Tina Martin, we were ushered into an impressive office overlooking the basketball facilities. I never would have guessed that Delaware had such impressive facilities. I viewed their program as a small, but up and coming one, though I knew it was benefitting from featuring one of the country's best players, Elena Delle Donne.

After the initial introductions and pleasantries, Coach Martin said, "the first thing we want to do is officially offer you a scholarship to attend the University of Delaware…The reason I want to do this now is so that you can relax, enjoy your visit (without wondering), and really try to envision yourself as a member of this program."

My wife and I looked at each other, thinking the same thing, "two offers in two days…wow this is crazy!" After a great visit around the Delaware campus, we headed back home to Massachusetts.

During our ride we tried to really focus on Jaylen and what she wanted in a school. We tried hard to remember that she was only in 9th grade. But things were happening so fast! We knew she had a busy summer, with showcase events and the one camp (Penn State) that she wanted to attend. We were careful to listen as she talked about the type of school she'd like, the kind of coach she wanted to play for, and the kind of teammates she wanted to play with.

Shocked and amazed by her mature and thoughtful answers to our questions – we began to probe further. We talked about everything, from what she wanted to major in to the style of (basketball) play she wanted.

Still, and I want to be clear on this, I don't want you to think that we were dealing with an incredibly mature 14 year old. Trust me, she's just like everyone else's kid. We yell at her to clean her room, do her homework, get off of social media and of course STOP TEXTING so much. She's an above average student, with an inconsistent work ethic. It's improving, but in no way exemplary. She's a normal teenage girl. I say all of this not to slam or degrade her, rather to let you know the basis for our surprise that she had gleaned so much from the years of school visits with her brothers. Moreover, I don't want you to think that we are dealing with an outlier on the maturity scale – and that her level of focus or interest are outside of your kid's reach.

After the drive home and a day or so to recover and reflect, we had a planned unofficial visit to Boston College. They had a new coaching staff, and had been (literally) "hounding" her coaches to get her to visit.

They had a full day planned, morning meetings with the coaching staff, meetings and lunch (on our own tab) with current and former players, meetings with academic staff and members of the training staff. As we toured the campus on this exceptionally hot summer day, we kept waiting for the magic words. Jaylen, we are going to offer you a scholarship. The words *never* came!

We spent a long 6 hours on the BC campus, thinking that an offer was sure to come; but it didn't. It was a great wake-up call for my wife and I. Still, something even more important happened. As we jumped back into our car for the comparatively quick 30 minute ride home, Jaylen said, "I really didn't want an offer from BC anyway." When I asked why, she said, "It's a city school on a small campus. I don't know how good their football program is (I will explain later.) I didn't care for the offense the coach described. They wear Under Armour and those shoes hurt my feet. And I don't think they've won any championships lately." *WOW!* I thought, she really did pay attention. Then, the last thing she emphatically said during the drive home was, "My only focus is going to camp this weekend, and earning an offer from Penn State!"

Shortly after we arrived on the Penn State campus, I began to notice something. I saw the same thing when Brennan visited UNC, the same thing I recognized when Camren and Armani visited Ohio State. There is an almost indescribable comfort level you will notice when your kid finds "their place". They operate with a different confidence and ease. They seem "at home". Whether or not they say it, you can tell that this is the place that they will not only survive, but actually ***thrive!***

From the moment she walked onto the court in the Bryce Jordan Center, she meant business. She did things that I had never seen her do on the court. She played with a confident swagger against girls who were 2 and 3 years older. "My gosh, this is their Elite Camp", I thought, as I watched her move with ease from drill to drill, and game to game against some of the top prospects on the PSU wish list. The coaches, pulled me aside and (jokingly) asked, "Can we have her NOW?"

As my wife and I returned to our hotel, we were still somewhat in shock from what we had just witnessed. Upon returning for the second and final day of the camp, Head Coach Coquese Washington asked us to meet with her after the camp ended. Then Assistant Coach Maren Walseth pulled us aside during the morning session and said, "Wow, we had a great time with Jaylen last night. We really got to know her, and she's the kind of kid that fits our program." No scholarship was yet offered; but we were definitely moving in the right direction.

As camp came to a close, we entered Coach Washington's office. She enthusiastically exclaimed, "Jaylen I am so impressed with how much you've improved since I last saw you play…We are going to offer you a scholarship!" As my wife clutched her chest in amazement, I choked back tears. You see, as a parent there are few things more fulfilling than to see your child set a truly ambitious goal and then accomplish it.

"Refocus, refocus," I said to myself. I know that this was her goal. I know that this is where she wants to be. We know it's the right place for her – BUT is she ready? I needed to talk to her. I had to slow this thing down. My gosh, it's my 9th grade, 14 year old daughter whose room at home is a mess right now. Is she really ready to make a 40 year decision.

Leaving the meeting, we agreed to talk it over as a family. Besides this, we thought it was necessary for Jaylen to discuss it with her high school coach and her AAU coach. After a few weeks to reflect, and review other offers that poured in over the summer – my wife and I gave her our blessing and permission to call Coach Washington and commit. No longer was she responding emotionally to leaving a loved one behind, she had found her place.

Home Visits

During all of these recruitments, it was always important for us to allow the full process to play out. The last phase in the narrowing down the potential scholarship opportunities was "in-home" visits by prospective coaching staffs. Visits are allowed as of the first Sunday in December. Assistant coaches are allowed to make as many *weekly* visits as they can schedule during that month. However, the Head Coach is only allowed to visit once.

As a family, we have had our share of visits from coaches expressing interest in our kids. One of the challenges with home visits is having someone you're used to seeing on TV sitting at your kitchen table. It's tough not to be overwhelmed by their dynamic personalities. Imagine, coaches that can all go by one name—Urban, Saban, Pitino, Boeheim, Auriemma, Coach Cal, or Jimbo—sitting in your home explaining why their school is the best fit for your kid. It's easy to lose sight that these guys are "professional convincers." They're really good recruiters and great at speaking to everyone in the room on an individual level. Beyond this, the best recruiters are impeccably well-prepared. They know each member of the family. They know things about your heritage, your religious beliefs, your family's core values and most importantly, they know who the key decision maker is within the family.

Of all of the visits our family experienced, no one came more prepared, or was more engaging than Coach Urban Meyer, from Ohio State. Although I should say that it's pretty easy for a coach to prepare for our family. Heck, my bio is online, and the *Cliff Notes* on my recruiting perspectives were in the first version of this very book.

Still, the challenge for the Ohio State staff was two-fold. They were both securing Camren's commitment and trying to convince Armani that OSU was the place for him. For convenience, we did the visit together – which further complicated the recruitment equation. There were two "connected" families and two individual players requiring two very different pitches.

Coach Meyer and his group arrived five minutes early. With him was Defensive Coordinator and Linebacker coach Luke Fickell, Co-Defensive Coordinator Everett Withers (who we knew from UNC), and Defensive Line coach Mike Vrabel, who was the primary recruiter for the boys.

I was initially impressed by Coach Meyer remembering the five minute conversation we'd had three years earlier, regarding Brennan coming to Florida. He said, "we missed out on one Williams kid, we won't miss on these two". Two things stood out in that statement. First, he remembered our brief chat. More importantly, he referred to Armani as a part of our family. He then proceeded to talk about life, specifically his life and how it had changed since his last coaching stint at Florida. With conviction, he addressed the impact that his association with Tim Tebow had on him. He spoke to the boys about their academic interests and how the academic advisory team at Ohio State would help support them. For the better part of an hour he spoke on these two subjects.

Then he turned the discussion to football. No offense intended, but it's tough to talk football in a room full of people who have very different levels of football knowledge. Understanding your audience is critical to successful communication. In that room, besides the targeted players, there was a former professional football player, the wife of that former player, the mother and aunt of a high school athlete, a sister who is herself an aspiring athlete, and another sister who just wants to hear about the school that her brother might attend. That is a tough crowd, to say the least!

You could see that the meeting was as planned and coordinated as any Saturday game that Meyer had coached. He gave an overview of the OSU football program, then Fickell and Withers took over. Since the boys played different position – both simultaneously and separately, Fickell talked to Cam about linebacker play, while Withers talked to Armani about defensive back play. Then Coach Meyer pulled the group back together. As the position coaches talked with detail and and some intricacy (keeping me and the boys interested), the Head Coach talked about body types and other more general things that kept the moms and sisters engaged.

At one point they turned our kitchen into a "make-shift" football field, with Camren at one end and Armani at the other. Coach Meyer explained to Camren how he would be playing with the best group of defensive linemen in the country. His confidence assured everyone that the defensive group OSU had recruited would be tremendous. He was speaking Cam's language for sure. Then he turned to my wife and said, "Jacquie, the reason Camren is gonna be great at Ohio State is (excuse me) – the guys with REALLY BIG ASSES that we will put in front of him." I have two REALLY WIDE ASSES that will be in the middle, and two MEDIUM SIZED ASSES that can really run, that will be on the outside of him." Without skipping a beat, he turned to Armani's mother, "Lisa, those two medium asses are gonna help Armani because they are going to make the quarterback throw the ball faster." In 30 minutes, they had explained their defensive philosophy at multiple levels – and we all understood what the system.

To close out the meeting, Coach Meyer addressed something that very few coaches deal with. He talked about "life after football." As any good "preacher" does he went goes back to his opening to set up his close. He talked about how football nearly cost him his family and (nearly) his life. He made the boys think about what and where they will be when the game ends. He tied in the value of the OSU degree, the power of the OSU alumni, and his plans for winning championships – "with good people, the right way!"

I should also mention that Urban knew he was following Michigan Coach Brady Hoke, who had visited the day before. In fact, Urban requested that (if at all possible) we make his visit the last. Somehow, this happened to work out with everyone's schedule. I have to admit that after Urban Meyer left our home, an old axiom rang out in my mind – "Nobody sings after Sinatra."

A few years before this, we'd seen this part of the process for the first time. For Brennan, we scheduled three visits; North Carolina, Wake Forest, and Boston College. There were several other schools that wanted to do an in-home visit which we declined. We just didn't think that they were under serious consideration. *Again, I emphasize the importance of being up front and honest with recruiters.*

Sunday night (the first night that in-home visits were allowed) we had our first visit with Head Coach Butch Davis, Sam Pittman, and Charlie Williams from North Carolina. They flew in on a private plane and were scheduled to arrive at our home at 6 pm. After meeting for more than 3 hours – the coaches left and headed back to the airport to return to North Carolina.

It was a great meeting. During the visit we talked football for about 20 minutes. The rest of the time we talked about our family, Brennan's other interests, the UNC School of Journalism, his prospective Carolina teammates, and churches in the Raleigh/Durham/Chapel Hill area.

On Wednesday, Coach Jim Grobe and Ray McCartney from Wake Forest visited. This was another great meeting. It lasted just under three hours. Wake also followed up this visit by sending Offensive Coordinator/Line Coach Steed Lobotske a week later. They did a tremendous job of presenting the school.

The next Sunday we met Head Coach Jeff Jagodzinski and Jack Bicknell Jr. from Boston College, who visited for about 20 minutes. I made mention of the duration of each visit because I started to notice that Coach Jagodzinski was not really enamored by the recruiting process. On Brennan's Official Visit to BC, "Jags" left dinner early and was noticeably absent during my son's time on campus. Parent's intuition is a key part of the process. Your life experiences may allow you to see things that your 17 year old son may not. I *was* surprised (but not shocked) when "Jags" stepped down and took a position in the NFL. Make no mistake, I think he's a heck of a college coach. What he did in his two years at BC was very impressive; but I don't think he liked the recruiting side of the college game. *This may in some way answer the question many have asked about how a kid from a Catholic high school in Boston would not be an automatic signee for a private Catholic college like BC.*

After the in-home visits it became clear, "crystal clear", that UNC would be the place for Brennan. Coach Davis made a statement during his visit that gave Brennan the *release* he needed to say yes to Carolina. He told him that he was confident that UNC was the best place for him academically, athletically and socially. Coach Davis also told him that he understood how hard it would be to say *no* to "other" people who had been so nice to him. "Saying yes is the easy part, saying no is tough," he exclaimed. "If you think UNC is where you want to be, here's how you say no to the others." The real question for Brennan was not how to say YES, rather it was how to say NO, and Coach Davis explained how he could say NO and not feel like a bad guy. Brennan really needed to hear this.

When Brennan chose UNC I was not surprised. I had developed what I refer to as the "sweatshirt indicator". After every visit, Official or Unofficial, I would ask Brennan if wanted to buy a sweatshirt from the school. He would always say, "nah, no, or not yet". Wake Forest and Virginia were close, he bought a t-shirt after visiting both schools. But as we were driving away from the UNC campus I asked if he wanted to get a sweatshirt, he quietly answered, "I guess so." Although he didn't admit it for a while, I had a strong feeling that he would be a Tar Heel.

As you go through this "narrowing-down" phase, I strongly recommend that you look for little signs like my sweatshirt indicator. They will tell you that your kid feels comfortable. Although they may not fully verbalize their feelings, there will be something different about *the school* your kid chooses to attend.

Sometimes the final selection process is easy, as it was Jaylen's recruitment, because your son or daughter may have always wanted to attend the school they choose. My dream school growing up was Michigan. Actually, I always thought that Brennan would go to Michigan; but it wasn't the right fit.

Speaking of Michigan, one of the toughest challenges I faced was not allowing my personal feelings to overly influence my kid's decisions. As a native Michigander, one of the first things you are taught, shortly after getting your first diaper changed, is to "HATE OHIO STATE". As I shared earlier, our family watched the Michigan-Ohio State game every year, always wearing blue, and always rooting for Michigan.

The first time I took the boys to visit Michigan, I jokingly made them take their shoes off. I referenced the Bible passage where God told Moses to take his shoes off, because he was standing on HOLY GROUND!

To help you understand the passion of this rivalry, I share this one tradition. When Ohio State travels to Michigan for the annual game they go by bus. The buses fill their gas tanks in Columbus and again in Toledo which is the last city before crossing the Ohio-Michigan border. They refuse to (even) buy gas in the state of Michigan. Furthermore the schools do not refer to each other by name. Ohio State calls Michigan, "the school up North." Michigan refers to Ohio State, simply as Ohio. Michigan's school color blue is forbidden in or around the Ohio State football facility. And both teams have a clock that counts down the 365 days each year (to the minute) until the two teams will play again. "Hatred" is a strong word, but it's applicable in this rivalry.

I give you this context so that you may see how it's necessary as a PCM to in some ways hold back personal feelings and opinions of the schools considering your student athletes, and the schools that your kids are interested in. You have to allow for an unbiased evaluation of the schools they're considering, especially when your own personal "Ohio State" in the final picture.

After removing your personal biases, the best advice I can give is, "Take your time!" The more time you take, the more you see, and the more clearly you see things. There were points in the process where I could have seen Brennan at any one of his final six choices. My mother used to tell me that it's easy to fool someone for a little while, but over time the real person (program) reveals itself. As the process wore on, we began to see the best fit and we are confident to this day that our son made the right choice.

After Brennan committed to UNC on national TV, I told Coach Pittman that he didn't have to worry about my son changing his mind and that he did not have to make the promised weekly check-in trips from Chapel Hill to Boston. Coach Pittman explained that although he was confident Brennan would stand by his word, he would still come each week to check on him. Because, as Coach "Pitt" so eloquently put it, "the deal ain't done – until it's done!"

A verbal commitment is simply telling the coach of your intended school that you plan to attend their school. You are allowed to verbally commit at any time; and when I say any time, I mean any time. Kids will commit when they are 8th graders, on the school's campus, or calling from home to tell the school the news. Since it's so easy to do, as in "Coach I have decided to attend your school," it's just as easy for a kid to change his mind and tell another school that same thing.

The "two-way street" of verbal commitments can come back to bite you in the butt. Two of my daughter's high school teammates saw the downside of early commitments. Her school's point guard committed to UMass-Lowell early, at the end of a great junior season. Shortly after her commitment she suffered a knee injury that required surgery and extensive rehab. After returning to play, it was obvious she wasn't the player she'd been prior to the injury. However, as she became more and more confident in her recovery, she began to play like her old self. However, the coaching staff at UMass-Lowell had already made the decision to rescind their offer. A week before signing day the Head Coach called to inform her and her mother that she no longer had a scholarship.

Jaylen's other high school teammate's unfortunate situation was a little more self-inflicted. Providence College offered her a scholarship after an incredible camp performance, the summer after her freshman year. Sound familiar? (See Jaylen's story.) She was a great student, Providence is a great school. It was the perfect fit. She committed immediately. After a solid sophomore season, her family decided AAU basketball was no longer necessary. Since she had already committed to a scholarship offer, they felt that the proverbial "hay was in the barn". They decided she had nothing else to do, nothing else to prove. A week before she started her junior year, Providence called and told her that her offer had been rescinded.

The worst part of the first case was the late stage at which they pulled the offer. The athlete literally was expecting to receive scholarship papers in the mail and was totally blindsided by the UMass-Lowell decision. She'd been off the recruiting market for more than a year, and had told other schools that she was fully committed to UMass-Lowell.

Devastated by the call, she licked her wounds and joined Jaylen's AAU program – The Rivals Basketball Club. Coach Scott Hazelton, met with her and her mom and put a recruiting plan together. Eventually she received a scholarship to Division 2 St. Michaels College.

The other young lady fortunately had more time to regenerate interest. The lesson here is that if and when your kid receives an early scholarship offer, it is not a guarantee. Secondly, when schools offer early, they are **projecting** that you are going to improve by the time you show up on their campus. The earlier the offer, the more improvement they expect. The last thing a school want to see is a committed athlete, "shut it down", or act as though they've arrived.

As I thought about Brennan's big moment on national TV – announcing his intention to attend UNC, I pictured the other finalists for his commitment (Wake Forest, Boston College, and Virginia) "sitting on the edge of their seats," waiting for this 17 year old kid to weigh in on their recruiting abilities. I remembered the story of Mike Siravo, BC Recruiting Coordinator, who told me that he literally fell off his chair, after being misinformed about a national TV announcement. I didn't like his description of such a scenario; so a week prior to the announcement, I called each school and informed them of Brennan's decision. Since we were dealing with first class programs, they all shared their disappointment and wished Brennan well. They all asked if they could talk to Brennan after he returned from the All-America game. I agreed to allow these contacts for two reasons; first, we had developed relationships with these great guys and I felt Brennan owed them an explanation. Secondly, I was confident that he had thought through his decision and would not waiver because of one conversation.

You Have Reached Your Destination: Signing the Letter of Intent

The first Wednesday in February is National Signing Day (NSD), the first day that high school football recruits can officially sign with the school of their choice. In basketball and some other college sports, an early signing period exists, and prospects can sign before their Senior season or a couple weeks after their season ends. By comparison, NSD is like a national holiday for college football fans. It is the equivalent of the NFL Draft day – when programs are built. In some cases, this is the day when as many as two to three years of recruiting a player finally pays off. It is also a day of huge disappointment when prospects who have verbally committed suddenly back out and sign with another program. This is probably the first real contract that your kid has ever executed. You should understand the binding obligations their signature holds.

Contrary to what many people believe, by and large, there is no negotiating an athletic scholarship. the top rated recruit gets the same scholarship as the last recruit on the list. And yes, there is a top recruit and there are lower-ranked recruits. In football, sources like Rivals.com and Scout.com *rate and rank* players in each recruiting class. Furthermore, they rate and rank each school's total recruiting class. You will hear terms like Five Star, Four Star, and numbers like 6.1, or 5.4. These sources pride themselves on their abilities to measure the quality of prospects, even projecting whether or not the player will make it to the "next level" (the NFL). The highest rated players carry the Five Star moniker. Of the more than 1 million high school football players there are only 25 – 30 Five Stars in any given year. There are about 200 or so Four Star players. The *renowned* ESPN also follows, rates, and ranks high school prospects, which shows the importance of this facet of the process. TV shows like *"Recruiting Insider"* and countless webcasts are built around following the recruiting process throughout the year. Rivals.com has even developed a satellite radio station that follows high school athletes and college sports.

There are thousands of man-hours that go into discovering, evaluating, recruiting, courting and coddling the high profile four and five star players. And it all culminates on NSD. Coaches are viewed as more valuable if they are recognized as great recruiters. Ed Odgeron, a highly regarded recruiter, moved from the NFL's New Orleans Saints to the University of Tennessee because of his ability to recruit "Johnny 5-Star." Odgeron is one of the highest paid assistant coaches in college football. John Blake at UNC, Corwin Brown at Notre Dame, and Penn State's Larry Johnson, are recognized as top-notch recruiters. There is an annual award given to the nation's top recruiter, based on a point system, for the number of top prospects they are able to sign. Blake, Brown, and Johnson are masters in developing relationships with players and families. I would add Brennan's lead recruiter, Sam Pittman, to the list. His ability to come in towards the end of the process and develop a rapport that made our family comfortable with Brennan's decision to attend UNC, is definitely deserving of such consideration.

The National Signing Day process is heavily regulated by the NCAA. Players are not allowed to sign before 7:00 AM EST to avoid unscrupulous activity. To further protect players, the NCAA has mandated a standard National Letter of Intent (NLI) so that additional clauses are not added. Brennan signed his NLI just after 7:00 AM, faxed it over to UNC, then drove to his high school for a ceremonial signing for the media and his school mates.

National Signing Day and the National Letter of Intent will be an exciting time for you and your family. Some players have parties; some have huge press conferences; some do "crazy" skits to make their surprise announcement. However you choose to do it, make sure you and your son understand the seriousness and finality of signing the letter. After signing, the athlete in many ways becomes "the property" of the university he has signed with. If he wants to change his mind and go to another school, it will cost him a full year of eligibility. So if your son is not ABSOLUTELY POSITITVE that this is the place for him, WAIT! You actually have until April 1st to sign as long as the school agrees to hold the scholarship. It is rare that players wait this long. However, if your son is highly regarded the school *might* wait. In past years, number of the country's top ranked recruits have not signed on signing day, both Terrell Pryor and Bryce Brown did not sign on the first Wednesday in February. Both citing different reasons, they nonetheless withheld their signatures until after NSD. Pryor eventually signed with Ohio State, and Brown backed out of his verbal commitment to Miami and signed with Tennessee more than a month after NSD.

Overtime: Your Work is Never Done

There are so many things that go into the Recruiting Process that I thought I should cover a few things we encountered separately. Although they may have fit into one of the *Four Quarters,* they deserve special attention because they speak to important considerations, special circumstances, and situations that may or may not apply to your kid's situation.

College Application Process: What do you mean I have to apply?

After the recruitment process has concluded, and your student-athlete has signed on the dotted line of the National Letter of Intent (NLI), you will receive a large package in the mail. The package we received included a two welcome letters, the strength and conditioning program information, a certificate representing the scholarship, and an application – yes, an application for admission into the school.

You would think that with all of the recruiting due diligence, admission into the school would be a foregone conclusion. Well it's not! Student-athletes still have to go through the full application process and get into the school that they have chosen. Although these occurrences are rare, there have been instances when a student-athlete has signed a letter of intent, but does not qualify for admission into the school. Schools that have very strict admissions requirements typically pre-qualify recruits using the early admissions process to avoid these embarrassing incidents.

Stanford, for example, pre-qualifies players before offering and then will pre-accept the prospect before he signs the letter of intent. Notre Dame does a tremendous amount of due diligence before a formal scholarship offer is extended. This is an attempt to ensure that the offer is not wasted. Duke puts players through a formal *one-on one* interview with the Director of Admissions to confirm the candidate's capabilities as a student.

The admissions scenario brings up an interesting aspect of the recruiting process. During Brennan's recruiting we tried to focus on good academic schools that had good football programs. There were several football programs we chose to stay away from because the school did not fit the basic profile for the type of institution we wanted Brennan to attend.

During the application process I learned that different schools have different rules. By that I mean, schools have different requirements for admission. Remember, no school is allowed to *reduce* the standards set by the NCAA (which are outlined in *Eligibility Center* section of this book.) However, each college we looked at had the ability to admit (or not admit) prospective student-athletes. Each school in Brennan's final 6 (really, final 7 with North Carolina) was ranked in the *Top 50 Colleges/Universities by U.S. News and World Report* over the past two to three years. Although each school offered a top-notch education, some of them had the ability to admit student athletes that may not have qualified as regular students.

For example, Boston College can reduce admission standards for a high quality *local* player. Wake Forest is allowed five or six exceptions for athlete admissions. Furthermore, schools like North Carolina and Virginia often recruit players who were sent to prep schools or attended Junior Colleges because they were not able to qualify during their high school years. The most impressive thing with these types of exceptions is that these schools all have outstanding graduation rates. *This demonstrates what a highly motivated person can do when given a chance.*

As you go through this process it is your job to "know your child" and be realistic! Everyone wants the best for their children, and sometimes wanting the best means that you have to say no. Just as important as it was for you to put him in the right position on the field, you need to put him in the right position off the field. When Stanford offered Brennan a scholarship, my wife and I discussed at great length whether or not he was the type of student that would succeed at a school like Stanford. Although we were both confident that he had the capacity to succeed at Stanford, he had not demonstrated, throughout his high school years, enough academic consistency to make us feel comfortable and confident that he would excel in Stanford's highly competitive scholastic environment.

We were flattered by Stanford's interest in Brennan, but in the end we felt the distance from Boston to California, coupled with the academic demands, might be more than he could handle. Brennan had a 3.25 grade point average in a mix of honors and college prep classes. But knowing our son and learning the expectations of Stanford, we felt he would be better served in a different academic environment.

North Carolina was the perfect academic fit for Brennan because, within his major, there was a tremendous focus on the subject area that he had excelled in during high school. Beyond this, the quality of the UNC education is enhanced by the diverse and sound academic platform they seek to establish in the first two academic years.

Brennan is a good football player! Brennan is good student! In my opinion Brennan would not be a good fit at quarterback, nor would he be a good fit at Harvard. Could he play quarterback? Sure! If Harvard was gracious enough to admit him, could he survive? Sure! But the reality is that he is a great fit as an offensive lineman and a great fit as a student at UNC.

The point of this discussion is that throughout the process it very easy to lose sight of the fact that your son is a student-athlete, not just an athlete. Although we were well aware of this, the gentle reminder we received in the form of an admissions application served notice that our son would have to be prepared for the challenge of fulfilling both athletic and academic requirements. As my college coach Dan Simrell told me after a great freshman football season and a poor first semester academic performance – "There is a reason you are called a student-athlete, and it's because you are a student first and athlete second." He further explained, "and if you don't become a better student, you will **no longer** be an athlete!"

Early Entry

A trend that is becoming increasingly popular is Early Entry into college. Through this process, a prospective student-athlete graduates from high school early and enters the college of his choice a semester earlier than the other members of his graduating class. The idea behind this strategy is to afford the player who graduates after completing half of their senior year, the opportunity to begin college in January and get a jump start, both academically and athletically, on that year's incoming scholarship class.

If his high school permits, a prospective student-athlete can thus graduate in December of his senior year and begin attending college in January. Although this strategy is not applicable for all sports, it is becoming more common in football. This allows the athlete to get an early jump on the demands of both school and football. He enrolls in college and gets a full semester under his belt before he would normally begin school. In addition, he is allowed to participate in off-season workouts and the 15 practice days of Spring Football. This can be a tremendous boost to the college acclimation process because most freshmen have to contend with both the introduction to campus life and a college football season when they enter during the "usual" fall admissions timeline.

The first time I heard about this concept involved a recruit from Ohio State, Maurice Clarett. Clarett was a running back who wanted to start school early with the hopes of leaving early to play in the NFL. He won the starting running back job during the Spring and had a great rookie year. He followed his great first year with another stellar performance in his second year. Things were looking great until he decided to challenge the NFL rule specifying that players are not eligible for the NFL (Draft) Selection Process until they have been out of high school for three years. Clarett's argument was that he had left school early and should be eligible to enter the draft. To make a long story short, he lost his college eligibility and his battle to play in the NFL, and after several bad (off-the-field) decisions has landed himself in prison. He has now become the "poster child" for the argument against leaving school early.

We chose not to consider Early Entry for Brennan because we felt that it would shorten one of the most memorable and enjoyable times of his life – his senior year of high school. This is the year where you get to enjoy the fruits of your underclassmen labors, the year of your Prom, and Pictures, and Senior Trips. Beyond this, at Brennan's school, the last semester of the Senior year is about giving back, by serving your community. Honestly, we were also (as parents) a little too selfish to consider allowing him to leave our household early.

KNOW YOUR KID! The reality is that for some young people, early entry, can be a great decision, and for some (like Maurice Clarett) it can have catastrophic consequences.

If you are considering this route as a football strategy for your son, you should realize that it's not something you decide to do during his senior year. This strategy is intricate and must be academically mapped out very early in your son's high school years. His school may require that he take extra courses or attend summer school to fulfill the school's graduation requirements. Or, as was the case with my son's school, "Don't even think about it!" That was the response from Principal Richard Chisholm, when I jokingly inquired about the prospect of Brennan leaving Catholic Memorial early.

As you can imagine, colleges like the idea of getting prospects in early and getting them acclimated to their system. In addition to giving the player a head start, it helps the college's scholarship count by allowing them to get an extra player and count him towards the previous year's class without costing the player any eligibility.

Here is the math. Remember, a D1 school can only sign 25 players a year towards their 85 scholarship maximum. However, if they can get two or three early entries they can sign up to 27 or 28 players because each early entrant will not count towards the incoming class count. So if a school has two or three additional scholarships available because of transfers, players leaving early for the NFL, or academic issues they can replace those scholarship athletes with players who are willing to start school early.

Late Entry

The opposite of the Early Entry process is the Late Entry. Most everyone is familiar with the term "Red-Shirt," the process in which a player practices and trains with the team during a given year, but does not play in a game and receives an extra year of eligibility. Few however, are aware of the concept of a "Gray-Shirt." A Gray-Shirt chooses not to enter the school in the fall with his class, but rather enters school in the January *after* his graduating class has begun college. This allows the school to push his scholarship count toward the next year's class. He simply doesn't attend school in the fall and joins the program fully in January.

Both Early and Late Entries are ways of allowing colleges to "over sign", meaning to sign more than the 25 scholarship players allowed by the NCAA. These strategies do not violate any rules or regulations; however, if the school recruiting your son commonly practices either strategy – you should ask how they plan to deal with the overage. More importantly, you have to ask the school if your son is a candidate for a Gray-Shirt, or Early Entry.

Prep Schools or Junior Colleges: Which Shoe Fits?

There are several reasons that prospective student-athletes attend Prep schools or Junior Colleges. The most popular reasons are: failure to pass the NCAA Eligibility Center requirements and lack of recruiting interest. In addition, players may choose one of these two academic options to increase the number of scholarship opportunities.

The concept of "prepping", particularly in football, has provided educational opportunities for young men all over the country and can be a tremendous resource in providing academic support to a young man who may not have had the appropriate resources and support during his traditional high school years.

As always there are those who will attempt to abuse the system by taking advantage of loopholes in NCAA regulations. You have to look at the Prep School opportunity from three angles; first, the angle of the student-athlete, second, the angle of the Prep School, and third, the angle of the College – as all three can abuse this process.

Student-Athlete

Some student-athletes view prep schools as a place to make up for the poor job their high school coach has done in marketing their talents to prospective colleges. Some student-athletes see prep schools as a pre-college situation that will help them improve their academic standing because of the "crappy" high school they attended.

Prep Schools

There are prep schools that look to bring in great football players who have absolutely no chance of getting to the next level. They use the player for their one year of prep eligibility and discard them. In addition, I know of one prep school that specializes in labeling kids "LD" – which stands for Learning Disabled, thus allowing the player to qualify for reduced standards when attempting to pass the NCAA Eligibility Center.

Colleges

There are colleges who use prep schools as incubators for their programs. They consistently oversign, then send the excess player(s) to do a year in prep school, with an "unwritten" agreement that the prep school will redirect the player back to their program *only*. Tuition at some prep schools can cost up to $50,000 year. Highly talented prospects *rarely* pay for the high costs associated with attending prep schools. Prep schools usually have large endowments or donors who financially support the football program by donating on behalf of the prospect.

Prep Summary

The prep school system was established to give kids a second chance – kids who were not able to qualify for college in the traditional manner, or kids who need an extra year to develop physically or mentally. The concept was not created for the aforementioned abuses; however, the loopholes open the door for corrupt activity.

I am all for giving more kids more opportunities. So, if the prep school route is something you're considering for your son – do your homework. Two years ago, I advised a player who had all of the measurables (6' 8" 340 pounds) to play D1 college football. However, he was a victim of his own academic laziness during his freshman and sophomore years of high school. His academic "light" clicked on in his junior year when he realized that he was going to have the opportunity to play at the next level. Unfortunately, too much damage had already been done and he was going to be forced to consider "prepping" or attending a junior college. He had five or six D1 offers that he would not be able to accept because he didn't qualify academically.

One of the schools that offered him a scholarship agreed to make arrangements to cover the costs of prepping, if he would agree to attend their school upon completion of the prep year. Two schools referred him to junior colleges that (as they put it) would only accept him if he would agree to come to their respective schools upon graduation. The schools actually had the audacity to suggest the only way that he could attend one of these junior colleges was if they recommended him – AS IF there are 6' 8" 340 pound prospects on every corner.

As we further investigated his options, we looked at prep schools. One prep school offered him the opportunity to enter the school under the "LD" tag, which would grant him lower standards for qualifying. During a very intense meeting where the "LD" tag was suggested, his mother became very emotional. The school outlined how they would have her son meet with a psychologist and that this specialist would professionally declare the student "LEARNING DISABLED". With tears welling up in her eyes, she continued to peruse his high school transcript. With a cracking whisper, she said "no, no that's not gonna happen." With tears streaming down her face she said, "my son does NOT have a learning disability." She further explained as she pointed to his transcript. His grades were terrible in the 9th and 10th grades, but during his Junior year he had a 2.8 and during his Senior year he was over a 3.0.

As her anger and frustration grew with the tone and focus of this meeting she came up with one of the best responses I can recall hearing. Glaring at her son she said to the coach, "my son is not "LD" he was just "DL." He was DAMN LAZY and now he has to pay a price for it." Furthermore, she said, "I am not going to sign papers that will follow him for the rest of his life."

Upon further review we realized that the damage from the poor performance coupled with the NCAA changes in the number of required Core classes (from 14 to 16), were too much for him to repair in a prep school, so we directed him to a Junior College. He currently has a 2.9 GPA and is on course to graduate a semester early.

If your son needs to prep there are a lot of reputable programs to consider. Make sure that you educate yourself on his options and understand the rules that the school operates under. Some prep schools are only allowed to take three or four post grad students, while others have no limits. In addition, understand the differences in academic support – as some prep schools do a tremendous job in preparing students for the SAT or ACT.

Just remember that the prep school system is not a bad thing. There are countless success stories. Still, you need to be aware of the potential for abuse.

Reclassifying

A strategy that has become increasingly popular is "Reclassification". Once a technique dominated by men's basketball – reclassifying athletes has spread like wildfire. Both male and female athletes are using this strategy in just about every sport. *Just imagine the obvious benefits – think of your student-athlete at their current age and proficiency competing against kids that are a year younger.*

Reclassification is the process where an athlete repeats an academic year with the hopes of improving their athletic and or academic performance. When the trend started most athletes would repeat their Freshman or Sophomore year – by transferring from a public to private school. Usually the academic rigors at a private school are more challenging – which legitimizes the repeat of the grade.

The NCAA's recent adjustment to how academic performance is calculated has changed the timing on when athletes repeat their grade. The NCAA used to allow a "double-dip" when an athlete that had repeated a grade would be allowed to choose the best **Core** course grades individually from the first attempt or the repeat year.

For example a student-athlete can choose to take the best grades from the first time he or she did the grade and combine them with the best grades from the repeat year. Combine the best of the two years provides a huge advantage. New NCAA rules no longer allow this double-dipping strategy. The athlete must complete their 16 core course academic requirements based on when they **enter** high school. Meaning as soon as you're kid enters high school they are on the "clock".

This new "clock" has made high school reclassification a less valuable strategy, and student-athletes are now reclassifying in middle school to avoid being on the high school academic clock. And trust me, by the looks of some of the kids attending our NextGen Camps, this strategy is being used a lot.

If you are considering this strategy be careful! Your student-athletes age may cost them a year of eligibility as most states have age limits for high school Seniors. Once again, do your homework before taking this path to college sports. One of Jaylen's former high school teammates lost her Senior year of eligibility. She started school late (age 6) and repeated her Freshman year, and would have turned 20 during her Senior year of high school which is prohibited by the Massachusetts High School Athletic Association.

Junior Colleges

As the prep school illustrations shows, one year at a prep school may not help your kid meet the NCAA qualifications set by the Eligibility Center. They may have to consider attending a Junior College (JC). In addition to meeting academic requirements, some players travel this route to improve their athletic skills in the hope of increasing the number of available scholarship opportunities.

Choosing a Junior College over a prep school means that in order to move to the next level, your son or daughter will have to graduate from the JC with an Associate's Degree (2 year Degree). In the best case scenario, they could complete his degree in 1 ½ years, which (in football) will allow him to enter the college of his choice a semester early, participate in Spring practice, and expedite his acclimation to the college environment. This strategy does not work for Winter or Spring sports because of the timing of the seasons and academic calendar.

The other significant consideration with Junior College is loss of eligibility. If your kid attends a prep school and then matriculates to a 4 year school, they will still have 5 years to complete 4 years of play. On the other hand, if he or she attends a JC, that time counts against their athletic eligibility at the 4 year school – giving them only 3 years to

complete 2 years of play. To further illustrate the aforementioned best case scenario, consider the following two situations.

172

Two Fall Sport athletes attend Junior College

(Assuming 4 Course Full Load)

	Player A	**Player B**
Summer School	Takes 2 Courses	1st Semester
Academic	Takes 4 Courses	Takes 4 Courses
Athletic	Fall Season 1	Fall Season 2
2nd Semester		
Academic	Takes 4 Courses	Takes 4 Courses
Athletic	Spring Practices 1	Spring Practices 1
Summer School	Takes 2 Courses	
3rd Semester		
Academic	4 Courses & Graduates	Takes 4 Courses
Athletic	Fall Season 2	Fall Season 2
4th Semester	**Player A:** Enrolls Early into 4 Year School	
Academic	Begins work toward 4 year Degree	
Athletic	Spring Practices at 4 Year School	
	Player B: Takes 4 Courses & Graduates Starts in the Summer/Fall	

As you can see by taking two courses each summer, Player A graduates a semester early and gets a head start on Player B.

Scouting Services & Recruiting Advisors

When I went through the recruiting process, more than 25 years ago, there were no Rivals.com, 247 Sports, Scout.com, Superprep.com, or other groups that provided the services of scouting and relaying information to college recruiters. These companies have grown to become integral pieces of the recruiting puzzle. If you don't believe me, ask Wall Street! Rivals.com was purchased for more than 100 million dollars in 2007 by publicly-owned Yahoo.com.

The life-blood of any successful football program is its ability to recruit good players. West Virginia Assistant Coach Billy Hahn says *"It's not the X's and O's, but it's the Jimmys and*

Joes that win." There is a high premium placed on the recruiting process and *reliable* information is extremely valuable. And, in an era where financial and human resources are limited, these outside recruiting services have become a vital conduit between the prospect and the program.

Because of their importance, it is critical that you become familiar with such services and how they operate. In the camp section we discussed exposure – well, these Scouting services are the people you will want to be exposed to. Is it important for you to know the likes of Mike Farrell, Bob Litchenfels, Matt Alkire, Tom Luginbill, or Jeremy Crabtree? If you son is a football player – YES! You don't have to have personal relationships with them; but you need to know who they are and ALWAYS take their calls.

During an interview with Matt Alkire of (formerly with) Scout.com, I was asked why Brennan (and our family) was so aloof in dealing with scouting services. He explained the importance of his role in providing information and that the (then) 10 scholarship offers Brennan held could easily quadruple if we would be more accessible to this facet of the process. I answered by saying that it was never our goal to get 30 or 40 offers, rather our goal was to find the right school. He replied, "how will you know that you've found the right school if you don't know all of the schools who may be interested." I guess I'd have to say "touché".

Matt was right! We didn't find the right school from the initial 10 offers, but when we opened ourselves up to the "scouting service" side of the process we increased Brennan's choices and eventually found the "right" school. A lot of schools won't admit they subscribe to the recruiting service information, but even those who say they don't, probably at least take a peek at the sites. A coach from one school, who vehemently denies ever looking at Rivals.com, quoted an article written on the website verbatim during a meeting with our family. I am not sure whether he wanted to give the site credit for bringing

Brennan to their attention or if he didn't want to appear lazy. I view it as maximizing your resources.

*While we are revisiting the subject of scouting services. it is important for me to address an important issue. Sometimes the guys (from scouting services) are accused of leading or directing players to specific programs – but it **never** happened during Brennan's recruitment. At one point in the process I asked Mike Farrell, "if he were advising Brennan, which school would he choose?" He explained that it was critical that he stay out of the selection process, and focus on reporting the news. He said that the moment that he crossed the line and became a part of the selection process, it would "forever" compromise the integrity of his company (Rivals.com), and possibly destroy the multi-million dollar scouting industry. I found these guys to be extremely professional!*

In addition to the key recruiting services like Scout.com, 247 Sports and Rivals.com, there are countless recruiting advisory companies that provide the service of matching your student-athlete to a college program that is commensurate with their athletic and academic abilities. In fact, because of my experience with Brennan, I have been asked to provide this service for several players and families that are seeking advice. Because I can't give the individual attention that these cases need – I decided not to attempt advising athletes. I will leave this task to the "professionals"

Recruiting Advisory Services

As with camps, (*and even more so*) "caveat emptor"! Some of these services charge a lot and do little. Out of curiosity, I contacted several companies to gather information on pricing and the services offered. I found a wide range offered in both categories. Pricing ranged from a couple hundred dollars to almost ten thousand dollars. Services ran from very basic and general advice, to detailed analysis, academic monitoring, standardized testing preparation, and comprehensive college matching. No matter what the price or level of service – the sales pitch was pretty similar. "Would you pay $_____ for a scholarship worth $200,000?" The problem with this pitch is that the advisor(s) can't guarantee you a scholarship, nor can they guarantee you financial aid to offset the cost of attending a school that doesn't offer scholarships, but does match your son's academic and athletic abilities with an appropriate school.

I firmly believe that there are prospects who go unnoticed and don't receive scholarships, but who have the ability to play, and may have benefited greatly from the services of a "reputable" recruiting advisory company.

One of the most highly regarded of these companies is the National Collegiate Scouting Association (NCSA), which provides a comprehensive approach to matching high school athletes to colleges in all sports. Although they do a great job – they don't guarantee anything.

I have heard both great reviews and complaints about their services – so I urge you to investigate these companies thoroughly. Besides NCSA, there are a number of regional and national companies that provide the same services.

Online Questionnaires

Almost all colleges have online questionnaires for their athletic departments that invite prospects to send in their information. To be completely honest, I am not convinced that they thoroughly review the thousands of completed responses. We completed at least 20 questionnaires and never received a response that I could confidently say was derived from the online questionnaire. Although I am not against using these online surveys, I would warn against using this mode of communication as the *sole means* of introducing your son to a program. Questionnaires are an efficient way to get your information to a school, but follow up with a letter, DVD, coach's recommendation letters, etc.

Insurance

A *revolutionary* concept that I developed for Brennan was the idea that he was an insurable interest – meaning that his written scholarship offer had a monetary value that could be lost if he were injured and unable to meet the physical requirements of playing college football.

One of the first written offers Brennan received was from Boston College. In their thoroughness, they outlined the value of a BC education. Furthermore the actually put a number on the value of a scholarship. The scholarship included books, room, board, and tuition and it was valued at $44,500.00. *Please note that a full scholarship is a full scholarship – in that they all cover the same thing. There's no negotiation. However, you should also realize that the cost associated with each school may differ, as the cost of a private school is usually more than a public school. The cost may or may not directly correlate with the quality of the education provided.*

That being said, I now had the ammunition I needed to prove that Brennan was finally (jokingly) worth something. In my profession, I serve as a Financial Advisor to professional athletes. One of the focus areas of my practice is disability insurance. Disability Insurance for professional athletes provides them with the comfort of knowing that if their career were to end due to injury, they would receive money to offset their loss. With professional athletes, it is very easy to put a monetary value on their potential exposure to loss, because it's written in their contracts. It is CRUCIAL for professional football players to have disability insurance because of the inherent dangers of the sport, coupled with the fact that football is the only professional sport that does NOT have guaranteed contracts. So, if pro players are injured and unable to play, the team is only responsible for paying them for the remainder of the season in which they were injured. When you hear of a player signing a 10 year – $100 million deal, realize if he gets injured during the first year and is unable to ever play football again, he could lose $90 million.

Because BC gave put a value in their scholarship offer, I was able to apply the same argument I use for my professional athlete clientele. If Brennan were to suffer a career ending injury he could lose almost $225,000 ($44,500 x 5 years). I used five years because that would be the maximum number of years that his education would be paid for.

After pulling together his medical history, and completing a short questionnaire about his high school football schedule, including the number of games played, games missed due to injury, etc. I received a letter from Lloyd's of London, Insurance Brokerage, stating that they would be willing to provide disability insurance coverage for his football-related activities. Being the consummate negotiator, I wanted more! My professional athletes have 24-hour coverage, meaning that if they are injured in any *legal* activity they will receive the benefit. So, if they were in an unfortunate car accident and injured to the extent that they could no longer play, it would be the same as if they had suffered a knee injury on the field.

After much debate Lloyd's agreed to the 24-hour coverage. The biggest concern they had was not football-related, it was that he was a young man who was a licensed driver. Moreover, in order to cover him in his off-field activities (mainly driving) they would charge us more for the insurance. I agreed to their terms and they sent me a bill for a "whopping" $1,300.00. That's right, I paid a little more than a thousand bucks to insure that he'd receive $225,000. I thought that was a pretty good deal. Thankfully, Brennan made it through both his Junior and Senior seasons unscathed – but my wife and I slept a lot better knowing that he was covered.

If your son or daughter has a scholarship offer and you would like to consider insuring them contact a Lloyd's of London licensed Broker and apply for coverage. Be aware that the Lloyd's Group are professionals and will not pay $225K to a family for their athlete's ankle sprain. Disability Insurance is a multi-billion dollar industry and Lloyd's of London knows how to value insurable interests.

Post Game: The Conclusion

As I complete the project of writing an addendum to this book, I realize that this has been a cathartic exercise, allowing me to relive the feelings, emotions and experiences over the years. I am reminded that it has been a blessing to watch my boys turn into a men and my little girl into a women right before my very eyes. I fondly remember both the positive and negative experiences we have shared along this winding road. I would love to take all of the credit for his accomplishments – but I am not the sole source of his development.

God has blessed my kids with the physical attributes required to play at the next level. Among other things, my wife has instilled in them a sense of humility that has allowed them to handle the attention derived from their success. Furthermore, there are countless pastors, coaches, mentors, and advisors who have made deposits into their growth and development as people and as a student-athletes.

In the midst of your journey I would strongly advise you to enjoy the scenery. It is the memories of the landscape along the road that will bring your biggest smiles. I shared with the parent of a player who I coached in my basketball program. The player was going through a horrible slump, and the parent was frustrated with me, as the coach, as well as with their "prodigy" for failing to meet their expectations. I explained to the father that if his entire career were equal to a full calendar year – this three game slump would be the equivalent of a "bad week". Don't let an occasional bad week spoil your year.

Remember that your athlete is going to have challenges and face obstacles that he or she may or may not overcome. I would encourage you NOT to remove those obstacles or eliminate those challenges. Rather allow them to fight through the test, for it is in those "fights" that your kid will grow to become all that he or she can be.

The best your athlete might become may be a D3 student-athlete. But if they love the game and wants to play at the next level, the tremendous college experience he or she has will not be a lot different than if they were at a D1 school. I believe that Nick Cataldo's experience as a football player at tiny Bowdoin College in Maine, was not be a lot different than Brennan's experience at North Carolina or Camren and Armani's at Ohio State. Sure my boys may have played on national TV, and I agree that more players from UNC and OSU make it to the NFL. But I still contend that athletes rule the world allows the "BMOC" (Big Man/Woman On Campus) feeling to transcend levels – and whether it's D1, D2, or D3, it's a special feeling to walk across a college campus as a member one of the school's athletic teams.

In closing this final chapter of the book, I realize two things. First, I am not an author – I am a football player, who became a father and was ignorant to a process that had drastically changed since my firsthand experience. Second, even in the midst of developing my younger son (Camren) – I had to educate myself in another arena basketball. And that would be, women's college basketball – as my (then) 5' 11" 11 year old daughter Jaylen was working to develop her hoop skills so that she could go to Tennessee like Candace Parker, Connecticut like Maya Moore, North Carolina or Ohio State to be follow one of her brothers, or where she ended up at her dream school Penn State, looking to blaze her own trail. I treasure every moment. I enjoyed all of the good times, and fought to make the best of the bad times. As I conclude the second edition of this experience my wife and I are fortunate to have had some incredible experiences – but nothing is more gratifying than seeing Brennan married with two children living his (second) dream as a WWE Superstar. Camren living his dream as a Scout for the New England Patriots, Armani working as a coaching assistant at Ohio State, and Jaylen growing as a player a Penn State.

Over the past 3 years I have poured myself into my NextGen All America Football Camps & The SHOW for one reason. As my wife says, "We are NOT having any more kids – so you need to find some other kids to help!" Nearly 500 Division 1 scholarship offers and counting,

At the ripe old age of 52 and nearly 20 years of coaching my kids, I still firmly believe **ATHLETES RULE THE WORLD!**

- AFTERWORD -

Now that you have read this book, I implore you to continue researching the recruiting process. It will be a tragedy if your son or daughter has the ability to make it to the next level and your failure to prepare costs them the opportunity. Don't make the same uninformed assumptions that I made in thinking that you know the process. I thought my experience as a high school recruit more than 25 years ago would be the same as Brennan's quest for the next level. I WAS WRONG! The road had drastically changed, and interestingly enough, continues to evolve. As the NCAA changes the rules of the game, you must be prepared to adapt at a moment's notice.

So get to work, continue to educate yourself and **I pray that you reach *your* destination safely!**

COLLEGE FOOTBALL PROSPECT MEASURABLE GUIDELINE CHARTS

DIVISION 1 PROSPECTS

Position	Height	Weight	40	Bench	Squat
QB	6'3"	200	4.6	260	425
RB	6'0"	210	4.5	315	415
WR	6'2"	185	4.5	235	315
TE	6'4"	240	4.7	300	440
OL	6'4"	280	5.1	320	450
DB (S)	6'2"	200	4.6	270	405
DB	6'0"	185	4.5	260	385
LB	6'1"	220	4.6	315	445
DL	6'4"	250	4.8	315	450

DIVISION 1-AA PROSPECTS

Position	Height	Weight	40	Bench	Squat
QB	6'2"	190	4.7	250	385
RB	5'11"	190	4.55	280	390
WR	6'1"	185	4.6	225	295
TE	6'4"	240	4.8	285	420
OL	6'3"	275	5.2	305	425
DB	6'0"	185	4.6	250	380
LB	6'2"	220	4.7	300	435
DL	6'3"	250	5	305	415

DIVISION 2 PROSPECTS

Position	Height	Weight	40	Bench	Squat
QB	6'2"	190	4.8	225	345
RB	5'11"	190	4.6	270	375
WR	6'1"	185	4.6	205	275
TE	6'3"	220	4.85	275	415
OL	6'3"	290	5.4	300	410
DB	5'11"	185	4.65	250	380
LB	6'0"	210	4.7	295	405
DL	6'2"	260	5.1	305	405

DIVISION 3 PROSPECTS

Position	Height	Weight	40	Bench	Squat
QB	6'0"	175	4.8	205	315
RB	5'10"	180	4.7	265	350
WR	6'1"	180	4.7	200	265
TE	6'2"	215	4.9	270	405
OL	6'2"	275	5.5	295	405
DB	5'10"	180	4.7	240	295
LB	5'11"	195	4.75	275	395
DL	6'1"	250	5.2	295	395

Source NCSA Recruiting Service – Check their site for your sport

NCAA SLIDING SCALE FOR D1 ELIGIBILITY

Core GPA	SAT (Verbal & Math Only)	ACT	Core GPA	SAT (Verbal & Math Only)	ACT
3.550 & Above	400	37	2.775	710	58
3.525	410	38	2.750	720	59
3.500	420	39	2.725	730	59
3.475	430	40	2.700	730	60
3.450	440	41	2.675	740-750	61
3.425	450	41	2.650	760	62
3.400	460	42	2.625	770	63
3.375	470	42	2.600	780	64
3.350	480	43	2.575	790	65
3.325	490	44	2.550	800	66
3.300	500	44	2.525	810	67
3.275	510	45	2.500	820	68
3.250	520	46	2.475	830	69
3.225	530	46	2.450	840-850	70
3.200	540	47	2.425	860	70
3.175	550	47	2.400	860	71
3.150	560	48	2.375	870	72
3.125	570	49	2.350	880	73
3.100	580	49	2.325	890	74
3.075	590	50	2.300	900	75
3.050	600	50	2.275	910	76
3.025	610	51	2.250	920	77
3.000	620	52	2.225	930	78
2.975	630	52	2.200	940	79
2.950	640	53	2.175	950	80
2.925	650	53	2.150	960	81
2.900	660	54	2.125	960	82
2.875	670	55	2.100	970	83
2.850	680	56	2.075	980	84
2.825	690	56	2.050	990	85
2.800	700	57	2.025	1000	86
2.775	710	58	2.000	1010	87
2.750	720	59			

*GPA's BELOW 2.30 MUST REDSHIRT

RECRUITING RESOURCE LIST

GREAT BOOKS TO READ

The Next Level – A Prep's Guide to College Recruiting – Joe Hornback

Meat Market: - Inside the Smash-Mouth World of College Football Recruiting – Bruce Feldman

Student Athlete Handbook for the 21st Century – Christine Grimes

Playing the Game: Inside Athletic Recruiting in the Ivy League – Chris Lincoln and Jay Fielder

ONLINE RESOURCES

National Collegiate Athletic Association (NCAA) – www.ncaa.org

NCAA Eligibility Center – www.eligibilitycenter.org

NCSA – www.ncsasports.org

Rivals From Yahoo Sports (Rivals.com) – www.rivals.com

Scout with Foxsports.com on MSN (Scout.com) – www.scout.com

ESPN.com Recruiting Website – www.espn.go.com

247 Sports – www.247Sports.com

Tom Lemming Report – www.tomlemmingprepfootball.com

All Star Girls Report – www.asgrbasketball.com

Blue Star Basketball – www.bluestarbb.com

Superprep Online – www.superprep.com

OTHER USEFUL RESOURCES

US New and World Reports Annual Report: Ranking the Top Colleges and Universities

NCAA Recruiting Calendar for your sport

RECRUIT MY KID!

A Parent's Guide Thru the Recruiting Process